Pizza

Pizza

AWARD-WINNING PIES
FOR THE HOME KITCHEN

Pete Evans

weldon**owen**

CONTENTS

PIZZA 101

I have had a very long love affair with pizza. It started at a young age when my mom would make pizzas on the weekends. My mates would come over to watch some movies and eat pizza after a day of surfing and kicking the football down at the beach. Mom would first make the dough, then top them with the best toppings she could find. The pizzas were quite simple and therein lies the beauty—you just need a few quality ingredients and the rest, as they say, is "as easy as (pizza) pie."

When I started my apprenticeship, at the age of seventeen, I was taught how to make "authentic" pizza by an Italian fellow named Arturo (or Arthur as he was often called). Arturo was a real pizzaiolo (pizza maker). To watch him work was like watching an opera, a ballet, and a rock concert all at the same time. Every part of the pizza-making process has a rhythm and feel to it, from the making of the dough, to the rolling out, tossing, and flattening of the dough.

It wasn't until I was thirty years old that I took on the biggest challenge of my culinary career and opened up a pizza restaurant. At the time, I had opened three award-winning restaurants that specialized in contemporary global cuisine, but I wanted to open a very cool pizzeria. I spent a year researching and working in pizzerias to uncover the secrets to the very best pizza. I can remember locking myself away for more than three months in the kitchen, experimenting with my pizzas. I would spend a whole day on the margherita, making 50 different versions of it. I would end the day completely and utterly exhausted, but having perfected the topping. I did the same with all the pizzas that made it onto the menu (and even on those that didn't). I wanted them to be faultless and, most importantly, they needed to be able to be replicated and recreated without me present in the restaurant kitchen. I believe I have achieved this and the restaurant has gone on to win numerous awards, including the Best Pizza in the World award in New York City in 2005 and also a few Best in Australia titles.

But awards aside, what I am most thrilled about is that I have been able to write this book with the knowledge and trust that YOU can create my pizzas at home for family and friends and, most importantly, for yourself, with the same results that I achieve in my restaurants.

As with all recipes, these are just ideas that work for me and my tastebuds, so I hope that they inspire you, and I encourage you to experiment with different flavors. I look forward to hearing about your culinary triumphs. (I am always thrilled when one of my readers sends me their success stories!) Send your top pizza toppings to info@peterevanschef.com. If you take just one of these recipes and incorporate it into your cooking repertoire, then I know that all the work that has gone into making this book has been worth it.

Cheers, Pete

A Quick History of the Pizza

Although well embedded in modern culture, the pizza, in its most humble form, has been around for centuries and originally would probably have been as simple as mixing flour with water and heating it on a hot stone, or even baking beneath the stones of the fire. After cooking, it would have been seasoned with a variety of toppings and used in the place of plates, or utensils when it would be broken into pieces to sop up broths or gravies.

It is widely believed that the idea of using bread as a plate can be attributed to the Greeks, who ate flat round bread (plankuntos) that were topped with seasonings and ingredients before baking. Being both thrifty and convenient, it was very much the food of the working man and his family.

Once this concept of plankuntos made its way to Naples in Italy, it started to develop into the pizza we recognize and love today. By the early nineteenth century, the first pizzerias were born to meet the growing demand and popularity of tomato-topped pizzas.

The pizza that really made a name for itself was the margherita. Created by pizzaiolo (pizza maker) Raffaele Esposito in a pizzeria in Naples to honor Queen Margherita of Savoy (the queen consort of Italy), the margherita was made using the colors of the Italian flag—red (tomatoes), white (mozzarella), and green (basil).

Fast forward a few hundred years and not much has changed. Italian immigrants brought pizza to America where it gained popularity from returning World War II GIs who had adored pizza in Italy. Different US states have made the pizza their own, with New York becoming famous for its thin-crust pizzas, while Chicago created the now legendary deep-dish pizzas.

Pizza is now one of the world's bestselling fast foods. But it can be so much more than the fast food that you pop down the street to pick up, or punch a few numbers into a phone to order. I honestly believe we should all be making it at home, as pizza is about fun, cheap, humble food that all the family can get involved in making, and the great thing about pizza is the variety of toppings you can put on it. They are almost endless.

My philosophy behind making a great pizza is very simple—less is more! You want to have wonderful toppings on the pizza that shine and stand out but you don't want too many competing flavors and you definitely don't want to drown it in too much cheese. Please keep in mind these pointers when making the pizzas in this book so that you can make award-winning pizzas too.

INGREDIENTS FOR THE PERFECT PIZZA

The Oven

The domestic countertop electric pizza ovens are brilliant as they can generate enough heat to make a commercial-quality pizza at home. This is because they have heat elements at the top and bottom, as well as a ceramic pizza stone, which helps to create the perfect crispy crust. The instructions for using this oven are on page 11.

A conventional oven, with the aid of a pizza stone (a flat piece of unglazed stoneware) heated to its hottest setting will also give good results. All domestic ovens differ, but as a general rule, the higher you place the pizza stone in the oven, the better the result. If you have a hooded grill at home, then crank it up as hot as it goes and follow the steps that I have outlined for a conventional oven. And, of course, if you're lucky enough to have a wood-fired oven at home, this will also do the trick.

The Dough

Making pizza dough is so easy; take the time to give it a go. You can store proofed dough balls in the freezer, then defrost when ready to use. It's fun for the kids and very cost effective. You need to use bread flour to make a proper pizza dough. In our restaurants, and in this book, we use dry yeast which we activate with lukewarm water before mixing into the dough. Next step is proofing. This is when the dough rests, giving it time to rise and for the yeast to ferment before baking. The ideal temperature is between 80°F (27°C) and 110°F (43°C). Any hotter and the yeast will be destroyed, resulting in a heavy and stodgy dough; any cooler and the yeast will not activate, resulting in an inferior dough. I roll out the pizza bases with semolina or flour as it gives the dough a beautiful crisp finish. I love a thin crust, so that I don't bloat my guests' bellies, but if you like a thicker dough, then by all means go for it. Finally, remember to dock the pizza (prick the base with a fork), to stop the dough from bubbling up when it's cooked.

The Sauce

There are generally two types of pizza bases, red (rosso) and white (bianco). Red is obviously a tomato base. My tried and true recipe for a tomato pizza sauce is the simplest thing in the world—I just take the best-quality canned, whole, peeled tomatoes I can find, then blend them with some sea salt, cracked black pepper and dried oregano—that's it! I don't cook it, I don't add garlic, I don't add fresh herbs, I don't use fresh tomatoes. This allows the toppings on this very basic, sweet, unadulterated sauce to shine. A white pizza consists of a simple olive oil and seasoning base, then topped with cheese so it doesn't burn, followed by the toppings of your choice. Don't drown the base in sauce or it will never crisp up.

The Cheese

In pizza making there are two types of mozzarella, the regular cow's milk stringy one, which is used on the base and acts like a glue to stick the toppings on. Less is more when it comes to this type of cheese. The second type is buffalo milk mozzarella, the food lover's choice. This is best added at the last minute, just before serving.

The Toppings

Splurge on the best-quality toppings you can afford. Go to a gourmet deli and invest in some paper-thin slices of San Daniele prosciutto or Parma ham—this will slightly melt as it is scattered across the top of a hot pizza. Also, pick up some sun-dried tomatoes, roasted bell peppers, and good-quality olives. And again, don't smother your pizza with toppings. Remember that what you put on after the pizza comes out of the oven can also turn a good pizza into a great one, so think about using fresh cheeses, toasted nuts, fresh herbs and herb sauces, dressings, and edible leaves of any description.

Buon appetito!

ELECTRIC PIZZA OVEN INSTRUCTIONS

Electric pizza ovens have a stone base and are specifically designed to cook perfect pizzas. Within each recipe, we've given instructions on how to cook the pizzas in a conventional oven, however if you have an electric pizza oven, here's how to use it for most of the following pizzas.

Of course, always refer to manufacturer's instructions before use. The care of the pizza stone is important so be sure to follow the manufacturers recommendations. Do not use parchment paper in the electric pizza oven.

COOKING INSTRUCTIONS FOR A STANDARD PIZZA: Turn on the pizza oven and preheat to the maximum heat for 3-4 minutes. Assemble the pizza on a lightly floured pizza peel or thin baking sheet, then turn the pizza oven down to the setting recommended for baking (consult the manufacturer's instructions). Transfer the pizza onto the preheated pizza oven stone and cook for 6-8 minutes. Turn off the pizza oven and remove the pizza.

COOKING INSTRUCTIONS FOR A CALZONE: Turn on the pizza oven and preheat to the maximum heat for 3-4 minutes. Assemble each calzone on a lightly floured pizza peel or thin baking sheet, press down the calzone gently and make three small incisions on the top of the calzone (this is to stop it puffing too much and burning on the element on the roof of the pizza oven). Turn the oven down to the setting recommended for baking (consult the manufacturer's instructions) and transfer one calzone on to the preheated pizza oven stone. Close the pizza oven and cook for another 8-10 minutes or until golden and crisp. Turn off the pizza oven and remove the pizza.

COOKING INSTRUCTIONS FOR PIZZA CONTAINING EGG: Turn on the pizza oven and preheat to the maximum heat for 3-4 minutes. Assemble the pizza, topped with all ingredients except the egg, on a lightly floured pizza peel or thin baking sheet, then turn the pizza oven down to the setting recommended for baking (consult the manufacturer's instructions). Transfer the pizza onto the preheated oven stone and cook for 2 minutes. Crack the egg into a cup, open the oven, add the egg to the center of the pizza, and season with salt and pepper. Return to the pizza oven and cook for 4-8 minutes. It's a good idea to check the egg at 4 minutes, and then cook longer as required as the egg can puff up. Turn off the pizza oven and remove the pizza.

PIZZA STONE

A pizza stone is a piece of unglazed ceramic or earthenware specifically used to cook pizzas on. The nature of the pizza stone and preheating it from a cold oven helps to distribute the heat evenly across the pizza base to create a crisp crust. Always put a pizza stone in a cold oven and then turn the oven on, letting it heat up along with the oven; adding a cold pizza stone to a hot oven can cause it to crack. Remember that once a pizza stone has been heated, the stone is too hot to handle, even with an oven glove. If you don't have a pizza stone, it is possible to preheat a large oven tray for 30 minutes and use it in the same way.

ESSENTIALS

DOUGH

The following three dough recipes each make one large quantity of dough, which can then be split into separate portions. Weights vary for the different pizzas you'll find in this book. Most recipes call for 6-oz balls of dough, but others call for other quantities, so consult the pizza recipe before you split the main dough into the separate dough portions. You can substitute whole-wheat or gluten-free dough for the classic dough in most recipes. (Please see note at the end of the gluten-free dough recipe for any restrictions.)

TOPPINGS

If you love making pizza, it's great to have a variety of toppings (like those on pages 18–21) in the pantry or the fridge that you can pull out and use at any time.

Classic Pizza Dough

In a small bowl, mix the warm water, yeast, and sugar together until combined, then leave in a warm place for 5 minutes or until frothy. Stir in the olive oil.

Sift the flour and salt together into a large bowl.

Pour the yeast mixture over the dry ingredients and use your hands to bring the mixture together to form a dough. Turn the dough out onto a work surface and use the heels of your hands to work the dough for 5 minutes until it is smooth and elastic.

Lightly grease the inside of a clean dry bowl with oil and place the dough inside. Place a dish towel over the dough and leave in a warm place to proof for 45 minutes to 1 hour or until double in size.

Dust a clean work surface lightly with flour and tip out the dough. Use your fists to knock the dough back with one good punch to let any air out.

Before you portion the dough into separate balls, refer to the pizza recipe you want to make for correct measures.

Once you've separated your dough into portions, and working with one portion at a time, use the palms of your hands to cup the dough and roll it on the work surface in a circular motion to form a perfect ball. Repeat with the remaining dough portions.

Place the dough balls on a lightly greased baking tray, cover, and leave in a warm place to proof for 15 minutes.

NOTE: Bread flour is very finely ground flour with a high gluten content. It is available from good delicatessens, gourmet food stores, and some supermarkets. It is sometimes called "OO" flour.

1 cup warm water

2 teaspoons active dry yeast

$1\frac{1}{4}$ teaspoons sugar

$1\frac{1}{2}$ tablespoons olive oil

3 cups + 1 tablespoon bread flour (see Note, below)

$1\frac{1}{4}$ teaspoons salt

All-purpose flour, for dusting

MAKES 26 OZ
ROUGHLY ENOUGH FOR FOUR
12-INCH PIZZAS

WHOLE-WHEAT PIZZA DOUGH

1 cup warm water

2 teaspoons active dry yeast

1¼ teaspoons sugar

1½ tablespoons olive oil

2½ cups + 3 tablespoons whole-wheat flour

1¼ teaspoons salt

Extra flour, for dusting

**MAKES 25 OZ
ROUGHLY ENOUGH FOR FOUR
12-INCH PIZZAS**

In a small bowl, mix the warm water, yeast, and sugar together until combined, then leave in a warm place for 5 minutes or until frothy. Stir in the olive oil.

Sift the flour and salt together into a large bowl.

Pour the yeast mixture over the dry ingredients and use your hands to bring the mixture together to form a dough. Turn the dough out onto a work surface and use the heels of your hands to work the dough for 5 minutes until it is smooth and elastic.

Lightly grease the inside of a clean dry bowl with oil and place the dough inside. Place a dish towel over the dough and leave in a warm place to proof for 45 minutes to 1 hour or until double in size.

Dust a clean work surface lightly with flour and tip out the dough. Use your fists to knock the dough back with one good punch to let any air out.

Before you portion the dough into separate balls, refer to the pizza recipe you want to make for correct measures.

Once you've separated your dough into portions, and working with one portion at a time, use the palms of your hands to cup the dough and roll it on the work surface in a circular motion to form a perfect ball. Repeat with the remaining dough portions.

Place the dough balls on a lightly greased baking tray, cover, and leave in a warm place for 15 minutes.

Gluten-Free Pizza Dough

Lightly grease a 12-inch pizza tray. Sift together the gluten-free flour, baking soda, salt, and sugar into a large bowl.

In a separate bowl, mix the eggs, oil, and water. Add to the dry ingredients and use a fork to incorporate, then use your hands to bring together to form a dough.

Before you portion the dough into separate balls, refer to the pizza recipe you want to make for correct measures. (See Note, below.)

Lay down a clean, dry dish towel and dust with the extra gluten-free flour.

Working with one portion of dough at a time, use your hands to gently press and flatten the dough as much as you can. Try to keep the dough as round as possible and then using a rolling pin, roll out to fit the prepared pizza tray. You will find that as this dough has no gluten, the dough will not have the elasticity of regular pizza dough and will therefore not be as easy to handle.

Lay your baking tray upside down on the rolled out dough and quickly flip it over, using the dish towel to help, so that you end up with a dough-lined pizza tray. It is now ready for the topping of your choice. Repeat with the remaining dough portions.

NOTE: As there is less elasticity in this dough compared to a regular dough, when a recipe calls for 6 oz, increase the dough portions by about 10 percent to $6\frac{2}{3}$ oz. This will help prevent tearing when you need to roll out the dough to fit a standard 12-inch pizza tray. The gluten-free dough cannot be used for any of the calzone recipes or the croque monsieur recipe as the dough is too delicate.

$2\frac{3}{4}$ cups + 3 tablespoons gluten-free flour

$\frac{1}{4}$ teaspoon baking soda

1 teaspoon salt

2 teaspoons sugar

2 eggs, lightly beaten

4 tablespoons extra-virgin olive oil

$\frac{2}{3}$ cup water

Extra gluten-free flour, for dusting

**MAKES 28 OZ
ROUGHLY ENOUGH FOR FOUR
12-INCH PIZZAS**

AÏOLI

2 egg yolks
1 tablespoon lemon juice
1 tablespoon white wine vinegar
3 garlic confit cloves, finely chopped (see p 20)
2 teaspoons dijon mustard
Pinch of sea salt
1 cup olive oil
1 cup vegetable oil
Sea salt and freshly ground black pepper

MAKES ABOUT 2 CUPS

Using a blender or hand mixer, blend the yolks, lemon juice, white wine vinegar, garlic confit, dijon mustard, and sea salt until combined. With the blender still running, slowly pour in the oils until the aïoli is creamy. Season with salt and pepper.

NOTE: Aïoli will keep in an airtight container in the fridge for up to 5 days.

BACCALA (SALT COD) SAUCE

2¾ oz salt cod, soaked in cold water for 48 hours, changing water halfway through soaking
2 tablespoons olive oil
4 garlic confit cloves (see p 20)
2 teaspoons chile confit (see p 19)
2 teaspoons onion confit (see p 20)
2 anchovies
1 tablespoon salted capers, rinsed and drained
1 tablespoon chopped pitted green olives
6 oz canned whole tomatoes (including liquid)
Handful of fresh flat-leaf (Italian) parsley, finely chopped
¼ cup fish broth
Sea salt and freshly ground black pepper

MAKES 1¼ CUPS

Drain the salt cod and break the flesh into flakes.

Heat the oil in a saucepan and sauté the garlic confit, chile confit, onion confit, anchovies, capers, green olives, and salt cod until fragrant. Drain the canned tomatoes and crush them in your hand. Add to the pan with the parsley and broth and cook over medium-low heat until the sauce has thickened slightly. Season with salt and pepper. Cool to room temperature.

NOTE: Store baccala sauce in an airtight container in the fridge for up to 3 days.

BALSAMIC REDUCTION

1 cup balsamic vinegar

MAKES ⅓ CUP

Pour the balsamic vinegar into a small saucepan and place over high heat. Whisk briskly while the vinegar comes to a boil so that it does not stick on the bottom of the pan. Continue to boil, whisking occasionally, until reduced to ⅓ cup. The vinegar will naturally sweeten as it reduces and will become syrupy. Allow to cool.

NOTE: Store in an airtight container in the fridge for up to 3 weeks.

PESTO

1 cup fresh basil leaves, firmly packed
2 garlic cloves
½ cup pine nuts
⅔ cup olive oil
⅓ cup finely grated parmesan
Sea salt and freshly ground black pepper

MAKES 1 CUP

Roughly chop the basil and garlic and place in the bowl of a food processor with the pine nuts. Process until finely chopped. With the motor running, slowly add the oil and continue to process for a few seconds until it forms a smooth sauce.

Turn off the processor and stir in the cheese. Season with salt and pepper to taste.

NOTE: To store the pesto, pour into an airtight container, cover the pesto with olive oil, then seal with a lid. It will keep in the fridge for 2-3 days.

PIZZA SAUCE

14-oz can whole peeled tomatoes
¼ teaspoon salt
1 teaspoon dried oregano
2 pinches freshly ground black pepper

MAKES 1⅔ CUPS

Place all ingredients in a food processor and blend until smooth.

NOTE: This sauce can be stored in an airtight container in the fridge for up to a week or in the freezer for up to 3 months.

SALSA VERDE

½ slice of stale bread
½ cup olive oil
1 cup fresh basil leaves, firmly packed
2 cups fresh flat-leaf (Italian) parsley leaves
½ cup fresh mint leaves
2 anchovies
1½ tablespoons capers, rinsed and drained
2 teaspoons finely chopped cornichons (small pickles), optional
2 teaspoons lemon juice
2½ tablespoons pine nuts, toasted
Sea salt and freshly ground black pepper

MAKES 1⅓ CUPS

Soak the bread in half the oil in a small bowl for about 5 minutes. Place the soaked bread in the bowl of a food processor with all the remaining ingredients and season with salt and pepper (being mindful that the capers and cornichons are quite salty). Process until finely chopped.

NOTE: To store, place in a sterilized screw-top jar and cover with a thin layer of oil, then seal with the lid. Salsa verde can be stored in the fridge for up to 5 days.

BALSAMIC ONIONS

4 tablespoons olive oil
2 large onions, thinly sliced
⅓ cup superfine sugar
⅔ cup balsamic vinegar

MAKES JUST OVER 1 CUP

Heat the oil in a medium heavy-bottomed skillet over medium-high heat. Add the onions and stir for 5 minutes, or until just starting to caramelize. Add the sugar and stir until dissolved. Add the vinegar and cook over low heat for 25-30 minutes, stirring occasionally, or until the mixture is a jam-like consistency.

NOTE: Balsamic onions can be stored in an airtight container in the fridge for up to 7 days.

CHILE CONFIT

5 oz fresh long red chiles, such as Anaheim or New Mexico, halved, seeded, and thinly sliced
½ cup olive oil

MAKES JUST OVER ½ CUP

Place the chiles and olive oil in a small saucepan over the lowest heat possible on your stovetop (use a simmer pad if necessary) and cook for 1 hour or until the chiles are soft. Remove from the heat and allow to cool.

NOTE: Chile confit (with the oil) will keep in a sealed sterilized jar in the fridge for up to 3 months.

Garlic Confit

This garlic confit is a favorite of mine. I like to use about 2 lb 4 oz of peeled garlic cloves and 4 cups of olive oil to make loads of it. Store as per the instructions given, then you've got some lovely garlicky oil to dress pastas, salads, and seafoods.

1 cup garlic cloves, peeled
1 cup olive oil

MAKES ABOUT 1½ CUPS, INCLUDING OIL

Place the garlic cloves and olive oil in a saucepan over the lowest setting possible on your stovetop (use a simmer pad if necessary) and cook for 1 hour or until the garlic is soft. You do not want the oil boiling at any time, you want it just past warm as this ensures the garlic becomes beautiful and soft—plus, you shouldn't get bad garlic breath if you cook it this way. Remove from the heat and allow to cool.

NOTE: The garlic confit (with the oil) will keep in a sealed sterilized jar in the fridge for up to 3 months.

If you are short of time you could roast garlic instead: Preheat the oven to 350°F (180°C). Place whole heads of garlic on a large piece of foil, drizzle with a little olive oil, and seal. Roast on a baking tray for 30-40 minutes or until tender. Cool slightly then squeeze the garlic from the skin.

Onion Confit

1 cup chopped onion
1 cup olive oil

MAKES 1½ CUPS, INCLUDING OIL

Place the onion and olive oil in a saucepan over the lowest setting possible on your stovetop (use a simmer pad if necessary) and cook for 1 hour or until the onion is soft. You do not want the oil to boil. Remove from the heat and allow to cool.

NOTE: The onion confit (with the oil) will keep in a sealed sterilized jar in the fridge for up to 3 months.

Peperonata

1 tablespoon olive oil
1 Spanish (red) onion, thinly sliced
5 tablespoons red wine vinegar
⅓ cup granulated sugar
1 roasted red bell pepper (see below), thickly sliced
1 roasted yellow bell pepper (see below), thickly sliced

MAKES 1 CUP

Heat the olive oil in a skillet over medium heat. Add the onion and cook for 1 minute. Add the vinegar and sugar and stir to dissolve the sugar. Increase the heat and bring to a boil. Remove from heat. Add the bell peppers. Allow to cool. Strain the liquid and discard.

Roasted Bell Peppers

1 red bell pepper
1 yellow bell pepper

MAKES 2 ROASTED BELL PEPPERS

Preheat the oven to 450°F-475°F (230°C-245°C). Place the bell peppers on a large baking sheet. Roast for 30-40 minutes or until the skins blister and turn black.

Remove from the oven and place in a bowl. Cover with plastic wrap or place the roasted bell peppers in a plastic bag until cool. Peel away the skins. Discard core, seeds, and membrane. Use the roasted flesh as desired.

NOTE: Roasted bell peppers will keep in an airtight container in the fridge for up to 1 week.

Tomato Chutney

1 tablespoon extra-virgin olive oil
1 tablespoon yellow mustard seeds
1 onion, chopped
3 garlic cloves, finely chopped
1 fresh long red chile, such as Anaheim or New Mexico, finely chopped
1 tablespoon ground ginger
1 tablespoon ground turmeric
6 ripe tomatoes, diced
2½ tablespoons red wine vinegar
3 tablespoons granulated sugar
Sea salt and freshly ground black pepper

MAKES 2¼ CUPS

Heat the oil in a small saucepan over medium-low heat, add the mustard seeds and onion, and cook until lightly brown. Add the garlic, chile, ginger, and turmeric and cook for 1 minute or until fragrant. Add the diced tomatoes and cook, stirring occasionally, for 20 minutes. Add the vinegar and sugar. Cook, stirring occasionally, for about 15 minutes or until the liquid has reduced by half. Season with salt and pepper, then set aside to cool.

NOTE: Tomato chutney can be stored in an airtight container in the fridge for 1-2 weeks.

Spicy Italian Sausage Mix

3½ oz ground pork
1 teaspoon garlic confit (see p 20), finely chopped
¼ teaspoon dried chile flakes, ground
¼ teaspoon fennel seeds, roasted and ground
¼ teaspoon salt
Good pinch of freshly ground black pepper

MAKES 3½ OZ

Put the ground pork in a bowl and sprinkle the other ingredients over the top. Mix well with your hands.

NOTE: This sausage mix can be made up to 2 days ahead of using. Store in an airtight container in the fridge. Or freeze (prior to rolling) in an airtight container for up to 3 months.

Meatball Mix

14 oz ground pork
5 oz ground veal
2⅓ cups coarse fresh sourdough breadcrumbs
3 tablespoons garlic confit (see p 20), finely chopped
3 tablespoons onion confit (see p 20)
½ cup chopped flat-leaf (Italian) parsley
¾ cup finely grated parmesan
3 egg yolks
1½ teaspoons salt
Good pinch of freshly ground black pepper

MAKES ABOUT 2¼ LB

To make the meatball mix, combine all of the ingredients in a large bowl and mix well with your hands.

NOTE: This meatball mix can be made up to 2 days ahead of using. Store in an airtight container in the fridge. Or freeze (prior to rolling) in an airtight container for up to 3 months.

CLASSIC PIZZAS

GARLIC AND ROSEMARY

I can remember my first dinner at an Italian restaurant. The first thing I tried was the bread they brought to the table, which was simply "garlic and herb bread." Wow! What a wonderful flavor. I thought bread up until that point was for sandwiches or toasted with honey, jelly, and peanut butter. And that's how this recipe comes into play. I love to serve this pizza as a start to a wonderful Italian-inspired dinner, or when mates pop over to watch football. It's cheap, and the smell that comes from the kitchen is intoxicating. Most importantly, it brings back those wonderful childhood memories of eating out at Italian restaurants with my family.

Semolina or all-purpose flour, for rolling

6 oz pizza dough (see p 15)

4 garlic cloves

Sea salt and freshly ground black pepper

3 tablespoons extra-virgin olive oil

½ cup shredded mozzarella

2 oz buffalo mozzarella, torn into pieces

4 garlic confit cloves (see p 20), cut in half

2 tablespoons fresh rosemary sprigs

MAKES ONE 6 X 12-INCH OVAL PIZZA

SERVES 1–2

Place a pizza stone in the oven and preheat the oven to 500°F (260°C) or to its highest temperature. Once it has reached the temperature, it will then take about 15 minutes for the pizza stone to heat up.

Lightly dust a clean work surface with semolina or flour, then roll out the dough into a rough 6 × 12-inch oval that is about ⅛ inch thick. Transfer the pizza base onto a piece of parchment paper; this is necessary for transferring the assembled pizza to the heated pizza stone. Prick the pizza base all over with a fork.

Finely chop the garlic, sprinkle with a little salt, then use the back of a knife to crush the garlic. Place in a small bowl with the extra-virgin olive oil. Season with pepper and stir to combine.

Spread the garlic paste evenly over the pizza base, then scatter with the shredded mozzarella, torn buffalo mozzarella, garlic confit, and rosemary sprigs. Season with salt and pepper.

Transfer the pizza onto the preheated pizza stone. Cook the pizza in the oven for 5-10 minutes or until golden and crisp. Carefully remove the pizza from the oven using a pizza peel or wide spatula and transfer to a cutting board. Serve.

MARGHERITA

This is the pizza that pizzerias around the world should be judged by. If they can't make a good margherita, then there is probably no chance of them doing justice to any other pizzas. It is the marriage of flavors of these ingredients that make this pizza stand the test of time. There are many different ways you can make this pizza, but remember the simple things in life are often the best, so make sure you use only the best-quality tomatoes, buffalo mozzarella, and basil (and, if you like, a touch of garlic or even chile). Crown it with sea salt and freshly ground black pepper.

Place a pizza stone in the oven and preheat the oven to 500°F (260°C) or to its highest temperature. Once it has reached the temperature, it will then take about 15 minutes for the pizza stone to heat up.

Lightly dust a clean work surface with semolina or flour, then roll out the dough to a 12-inch round that is ⅛ inch thick. Transfer the pizza base onto a piece of parchment paper; this is necessary for transferring the assembled pizza to the heated pizza stone. Prick the pizza base all over with a fork.

Spread the pizza base evenly with the pizza sauce, then scatter over the parsley and shredded mozzarella. Place the tomato slices over the pizza and scatter over the garlic. Season with salt and pepper.

Transfer the pizza onto the preheated pizza stone. Cook the pizza in the oven for 3-5 minutes, then place the torn buffalo mozzarella on the pizza and cook for a further 3-5 minutes or until golden and crisp. Carefully remove the pizza from the oven using a pizza peel or wide spatula and transfer to a cutting board. Sprinkle the hot pizza with the basil and parmesan, and serve.

Semolina or all-purpose flour, for rolling

6 oz pizza dough (see p 15)

⅓ cup pizza sauce (see p 19)

1 tablespoon chopped fresh flat-leaf (Italian) parsley

½ cup shredded mozzarella

2 very ripe heirloom tomatoes, thickly sliced

1 tablespoon garlic confit (see p 20), crushed

Sea salt and freshly ground black pepper

1 oz buffalo mozzarella, torn into pieces

12 fresh basil leaves

1 tablespoon finely grated parmesan cheese

MAKES ONE 12-INCH ROUND PIZZA

SERVES 1–2

Four Cheese

My secret for coming up with a good pizza topping is to think about what works as a pasta sauce, then use those same flavors as a pizza topping. This works most of the time, however nothing explains how the ham and pineapple pizza came about, as I can only cringe to think about that as a pasta dish. This classic four-cheese combination works really well as a sauce for gnocchi or pasta, but I think its best use is for topping a pizza. Because of the richness of the cheese, I wouldn't recommend eating this every week—I can hear my dad saying to me: "Everything in moderation, Pete." Take his advice and serve this pizza as part of a greater meal when everyone can have just one slice.

Semolina or all-purpose flour, for rolling

2 × 3-oz pizza doughs (see p 15)

2 tablespoons extra-virgin olive oil

1 oz taleggio or fontina

1 oz gorgonzola

2 oz buffalo mozzarella, torn

2 tablespoons finely grated parmesan

Sea salt and freshly ground black pepper

¼ cup vegetable oil

8 fresh sage leaves

1 oz walnuts, toasted and chopped, optional

MAKES TWO 6-INCH ROUND PIZZAS

SERVES 1–2

Place two pizza stones in the oven and preheat the oven to 500°F (260°C) or to its highest temperature. Once it has reached the temperature, it will then take about 15 minutes for the pizza stones to heat up.

Lightly dust a clean work surface with semolina or flour, then roll out the dough into two 6-inch rounds that are about ⅛ inch thick. Transfer the pizza bases onto squares of parchment paper; this is necessary for transferring the assembled pizzas to the heated pizza stones. Prick the pizza bases all over with a fork.

Brush the pizza bases with olive oil, then crumble the taleggio and gorgonzola on top. Sprinkle with the buffalo mozzarella and parmesan. Season with salt and pepper.

Transfer the pizzas onto the preheated pizza stones. Cook the pizzas in the oven for 5-10 minutes or until golden and crisp.

Meanwhile, heat the vegetable oil in a small saucepan over medium-high heat. Add the sage leaves and cook for 30-60 seconds until crisp. Remove with a slotted spoon and drain on a paper towel.

Carefully remove the pizzas from the oven using a pizza peel or wide spatula and transfer to a cutting board. Sprinkle with the walnuts, if using, and fried sage leaves. Serve.

Italian Meatball

Nothing brings back childhood memories like eating this pizza. As a kid I used to watch my mom making meatballs in the kitchen and she seemed so happy making them, with a glass of red wine at hand and music playing. This pizza marries children's two loves: pizza and meatballs.

Place two pizza stones in the oven. Preheat the oven to 350°F (180°C). Divide the meatball mix into 24 portions of about 1 tablespoon each, then roll into meatballs. Place the meatballs on a baking tray, drizzle with a little oil, and cook in the oven for 10 minutes or until cooked through.

Increase the oven temperature to 500°F (260°C) or to its highest temperature. Once it has reached the temperature, it will then take about 15 minutes for the pizza stones to heat up.

Lightly dust a clean work surface with semolina or flour, then roll out each dough into 6-inch rounds that are about 1/8 inch thick. Transfer the pizza bases onto squares of parchment paper; this is necessary for transferring the assembled pizzas to the heated pizza stones. Prick the pizza bases all over with a fork.

Spread two-thirds of the pizza sauce evenly over the four pizza bases, then scatter the shredded mozzarella, meatballs, torn buffalo mozzarella, and torn basil evenly over the pizzas. Season with salt and pepper.

Transfer two of the pizzas onto the preheated pizza stones. Cook the pizzas in the oven for 5-10 minutes or until golden and crisp. Meanwhile, to make the cherry tomato salad, place the garlic and oil in a saucepan over low heat. Cook until the garlic just turns golden, then take off the heat. Place the tomatoes, oregano, and vinegar in a bowl and season with salt and pepper. While the garlic is hot, pour it, along with the oil, over the tomato salad and gently mix to combine.

Carefully remove the pizzas from the oven using a pizza peel or wide spatula and transfer to serving plates. Cook the remaining two pizzas. Spoon the remaining pizza sauce over the meatballs on the four pizzas and top with some of the tomato salad. Scatter with the shaved parmesan and serve.

17 oz meatball mix (see p 21)

Olive oil, for drizzling

Semolina or all-purpose flour, for rolling

4 × 3-oz pizza doughs (see p 15)

1 cup pizza sauce (see p 19)

1 cup shredded mozzarella

2 oz buffalo mozzarella, torn into pieces

16 fresh basil leaves, torn

Sea salt and freshly ground black pepper

Shaved parmesan, to serve

Cherry Tomato Salad

2 garlic cloves, thinly sliced

1/3 cup olive oil

10 cherry tomatoes, cut in half

2 tablespoons fresh oregano, coarsely chopped

1 tablespoon red wine vinegar

Sea salt and freshly ground black pepper

MAKES FOUR 6-INCH ROUND PIZZAS

SERVES 1–2

Spinach with Feta, Olives, and Sun-Dried Tomatoes

If Popeye had made a pizza, I think this is the one he would have created. This was on the menu at a good mate's pizza store just up the road from where I lived, called Doughboy. The owner, Tony, was generous enough to let me work in his store before I opened up my own restaurant, so that I could see exactly how a good pizza store was run. This was my favorite pizza at Doughboy, so I thought it would be a crime to leave it out of this pizza book. Thanks, Tony!

Olive oil, for drizzling

5 oz baby spinach, washed and stems removed

Sea salt and freshly ground black pepper

Semolina or all-purpose flour, for rolling

6 oz pizza dough (see p 15)

⅓ cup pizza sauce (see p 19)

9 pitted kalamata olives, cut in half

½ cup shredded mozzarella

1 oz feta cheese, crumbled

1 teaspoon dried chile flakes

10 sun-dried tomatoes, cut into strips

Squeeze of lemon, to serve

MAKES ONE 12-INCH ROUND PIZZA

SERVES 1–2

Heat a skillet with a touch of oil over medium heat; when hot, add the spinach. Season with salt and pepper and cook until wilted. Place the wilted spinach on a clean dish towel to remove any excess water.

Place a pizza stone in the oven and preheat the oven to 500°F (260°C) or to its highest temperature. Once it has reached the temperature, it will then take about 15 minutes for the pizza stone to heat up.

Lightly dust a clean work surface with semolina or flour, then roll out the dough into a 12-inch round that is ⅛ inch thick. Transfer the pizza base onto a piece of parchment paper; this is necessary for transferring the assembled pizza to the heated pizza stone. Prick the pizza base all over with a fork.

Spread the pizza sauce evenly over the pizza base, then spread the spinach over the top. Add the olives and scatter over the mozzarella and crumbled feta. Finish with the dried chile flakes and a drizzle of olive oil. Season to taste with salt and pepper.

Transfer the pizza onto the preheated pizza stone. Cook the pizza in the oven for 5-10 minutes or until golden and crisp. Carefully remove the pizza from the oven using a pizza peel or wide spatula and transfer to a cutting board.

Scatter the sun-dried tomato strips over the pizza and serve with a good squeeze of lemon.

EGGPLANT AND SMOKED MOZZARELLA WITH CAPONATA

These simple, elegant ingredients make a totally sublime pizza.

Preheat the broiler to medium. Line a baking sheet with foil. Place the eggplant slices on the baking sheet, brush with olive oil and sprinkle lightly with salt. Broil the eggplant until lightly golden and tender (keep a close eye on it). You are just broiling one side of the eggplant. Set aside.

To make the caponata, preheat a deep-fryer to 350°F (180°C) or a large, deep, heavy-bottomed saucepan filled with oil to a depth of 2 inches. Add the diced eggplant to the deep-fryer or saucepan and cook for 3 minutes or until the eggplant is golden. Drain on paper towels. In the same oil, deep-fry the onion for 2 minutes until golden brown. Drain on a paper towel and allow to cool. Once cooled, add to a bowl along with the eggplant, parsley, anchovy (optional), tomato, and vinegar. Season with salt and pepper. Set aside.

Place a pizza stone in the oven and preheat the oven to 500°F (260°C) or to its highest temperature. Once it has reached the temperature, it will then take about 15 minutes for the pizza stone to heat up.

Lightly dust a clean work surface with semolina or flour, then roll out the dough into a 10 × 12-inch rectangle that is about ⅛ inch thick. Transfer the pizza base onto a piece of parchment paper; this is necessary for transferring the assembled pizza to the heated pizza stone. Prick the pizza base all over with a fork.

Spread the pizza base with the pizza sauce, basil leaves, sliced tomato, grilled eggplant, shredded mozzarella, and smoked mozzarella. Sprinkle with chile flakes and season with salt and pepper.

Transfer the pizza onto the preheated pizza stone. Cook the pizza in the oven for 5-10 minutes or until golden and crisp. Carefully remove the pizza from the oven using a pizza peel or wide spatula and transfer to a cutting board. Scatter the caponata on top of the pizza and serve.

¼ eggplant, thinly sliced

¼ cup olive oil

Sea salt and freshly ground black pepper

Semolina or all-purpose flour, for rolling

6 oz pizza dough (see p 15)

⅓ cup pizza sauce (see p 19)

8 large fresh basil leaves

1 ripe roma tomato, cut into ¼-inch-thick slices

¼ cup shredded mozzarella

2 oz smoked mozzarella (scamorza) cheese, torn into pieces

Dried chile flakes, to serve

CAPONATA

Vegetable oil, for deep-frying

¼ eggplant, diced

¼ onion, diced

¼ tablespoon chopped fresh flat-leaf (Italian) parsley

1 anchovy fillet, finely chopped, optional

½ ripe roma tomato, seeded and finely diced

1 tablespoon red wine vinegar

Sea salt and freshly ground black pepper

MAKES ONE 10 X 12-INCH RECTANGLE PIZZA

SERVES 1–2

Potato and Rosemary

This is a strange pizza. As a rule of thumb, when cooking, you never usually combine two starches together in a dish where the main component is a starch, so it came as some surprise when I took a bite of my first potato pizza and discovered what a beautiful combination it created. The secret here is to add aromatic rosemary and salty anchovies to really enliven the subtleness of the paper-thin potato. And if you don't like anchovies, you can simply add some extra sea salt or olives. Also terrific with slices of leftover roast lamb or pork.

½ large red-skinned potato, skin on

Semolina or all-purpose flour, for rolling

6 oz pizza dough (see p 15)

1 tablespoon olive oil

½ cup fresh ricotta cheese

1 tablespoon garlic confit (see page 20), finely chopped

⅓ cup balsamic onion (see p 19)

½ cup shredded mozzarella

1½ oz buffalo mozzarella, torn

2 sprigs fresh rosemary, leaves picked

Sea salt and freshly ground black pepper

6 white anchovies, optional

MAKES ONE 12-INCH ROUND PIZZA

SERVES 1–2

Thinly slice the potato, then plunge the slices into a saucepan of salted boiling water for 45 seconds. Drain in a colander and refresh immediately in cold water. Drain again, then lay out on a clean dish towel to dry.

Place a pizza stone in the oven and preheat the oven to 500°F (260°C) or to its highest temperature. Once it has reached the temperature, it will then take about 15 minutes for the pizza stone to heat up.

Lightly dust a clean work surface with semolina or flour, then roll out the dough into a 12-inch round that is ⅛ inch thick. Transfer the pizza base onto a piece of parchment paper; this is necessary for transferring the assembled pizza to the heated pizza stone. Prick the pizza base all over with a fork. Brush with the olive oil.

In a small bowl, mix the ricotta cheese and garlic confit. Spread over the pizza base leaving a ¼-inch edge. Scatter the balsamic onion over the top, followed by the shredded mozzarella.

Starting from the outside edge of the pizza base and slightly overlapping the slices, add the potato. Brush with olive oil before cooking. Top with the buffalo mozzarella and rosemary. Season to taste with salt and pepper.

Transfer the pizza onto the preheated pizza stone. Cook the pizza in the oven for 5-10 minutes or until golden and crisp. Carefully remove the pizza from the oven using a pizza peel or wide spatula and transfer to a cutting board. Top with the anchovies, if using, and serve.

MUSHROOM WITH BALSAMIC ONION AND TALEGGIO

Each year in fall, I go mushroom picking. What a joy it is to pick them, but even more so is the joy to cook with them and finally eat them. You can use any type of mushroom for this pizza—I've used field mushrooms. Top with just enough taleggio so you don't overpower the mushroom flavor.

Place a pizza stone in the oven.

To make the mushroom duxelle, preheat the oven to 350°F (180°C). Place the mushrooms in a small baking tray, drizzle with half the olive oil, and roast for 8 minutes. Remove from the oven (leaving the oven still on), allow to cool slightly, then purée in a small food processor. Fold in the remaining oil, thyme, and truffle paste, if using. Set aside.

Place the mushrooms on a small baking sheet, drizzle with the olive oil, and roast for 8 minutes or until tender. Thinly slice the mushrooms.

Increase the oven temperature to 500°F (260°C) or to its highest temperature. Once it has reached the temperature, it will then take about 15 minutes for the pizza stone to heat up.

Lightly dust a clean work surface with semolina or flour, then roll out the dough into a rough 10 × 12-inch rectangle that is ⅛ inch thick. Transfer the pizza base onto a piece of parchment paper; this is necessary for transferring the assembled pizza to the heated pizza stone. Prick the pizza base all over with a fork.

Spread the mushroom duxelle evenly over the pizza base. Scatter over the parsley, sliced mushrooms, balsamic onion, shredded and buffalo mozzarella cheeses, taleggio, and thyme. Season with salt and pepper. Transfer the pizza onto the preheated pizza stone. Cook the pizza in the oven for 5-10 minutes or until golden and crisp. Carefully remove the pizza from the oven using a pizza peel or wide spatula and transfer to a wire rack. Sprinkle with lemon zest and serve.

2 large field mushrooms, such as Portobellos (3½ oz total)

1 tablespoon olive oil

Semolina or all-purpose flour, for rolling

6 oz pizza dough (see p 15)

1 tablespoon fresh flat-leaf (Italian) parsley, torn

1 tablespoon balsamic onion (see p 19)

½ cup shredded mozzarella

2 oz buffalo mozzarella, torn

1½ oz taleggio, broken into chunks

1 tablespoon fresh thyme leaves

Salt and freshly ground black pepper

Finely grated zest of ½ lemon

MUSHROOM DUXELLE

2 large field mushrooms, such as Portobellos (3½ oz total)

2 tablespoons extra-virgin olive oil

2 teaspoons fresh thyme leaves, chopped

1 tablespoon truffle paste, optional

MAKES ONE 10 X 12-INCH RECTANGLE PIZZA

SERVES 1–2

Prosciutto with Arugula and Parmesan

This is the most popular pizza at my restaurants and it's the simplest to make. The beauty of this lies in the fabulously fresh ingredients that adorn the pizza once it has come out of the oven. You need the best-quality prosciutto or Spanish jamón sliced as thinly as possible so that you can see through it. Add to that some peppery arugula leaves and superior-quality Parmigiano Reggiano that you can either shave or finely grate. Some people like to cook the prosciutto on the pizza, which is fine, however I like to put it on the pizza as soon as it comes from the oven so that the fat on the prosciutto dissolves into the pizza and it is wonderfully delicate instead of being crisp.

Semolina or all-purpose flour, for rolling

6 oz pizza dough (see p 15)

⅓ cup pizza sauce (see p 19)

½ cup shredded mozzarella

8 fresh basil leaves, torn

1 roma tomato, cut into 8 slices

1 oz buffalo mozzarella, torn

Sea salt and freshly ground black pepper

1 tablespoon balsamic vinegar

2 tablespoons extra-virgin olive oil

Handful of large arugula leaves, washed and dried

6 thin slices prosciutto, preferably San Daniele

Shaved parmesan, to serve

MAKES ONE 12-INCH ROUND PIZZA

SERVES 1–2

Place a pizza stone in the oven and preheat the oven to 500°F (260°C) or to its highest temperature. Once it has reached the temperature, it will then take about 15 minutes for the pizza stone to heat up.

Lightly dust a clean work surface with semolina or flour, then roll out the dough into a 12-inch round that is ⅛ inch thick. Transfer the pizza base onto a piece of parchment paper; this is necessary for transferring the assembled pizza to the heated pizza stone. Prick the pizza base all over with a fork.

Spread the pizza sauce evenly over the pizza base. Scatter over the shredded mozzarella followed by the torn basil, sliced tomato, and buffalo mozzarella. Season with salt and pepper.

Transfer the pizza onto the preheated pizza stone. Cook the pizza in the oven for 5-10 minutes or until golden and crisp. Carefully remove the pizza from the oven using a pizza peel or wide spatula and transfer to a cutting board.

Meanwhile, whisk together the vinegar and olive oil in a small bowl and season with salt and pepper. Dress the arugula with the balsamic dressing and toss until coated.

Scatter the dressed arugula neatly over the cooked pizza, then lay slices of prosciutto over the top. Serve scattered with the parmesan.

PEPPERONI WITH CHILE

This is my all-time favorite pizza. I love the chewiness of the pepperoni and also the heat that comes from the chile in it. There is a classic Italian combination that combines chile and mint and I really wanted to see what that was like on a pizza, so I tried it with the pepperoni and discovered it works great. The buffalo mozzarella adds a wonderful creaminess to the pizza that ties it all together. If you want to keep it simple, by all means omit the mint, but do me a favor and try it at least once.

Place a pizza stone in the oven and preheat the oven to 500°F (260°C) or to its highest temperature. Once it has reached the temperature, it will then take about 15 minutes for the pizza stone to heat up.

Lightly dust a clean work surface with semolina or flour, then roll out the dough into a 12-inch round that is ⅛ inch thick. Transfer the pizza base onto a piece of parchment paper; this is necessary for transferring the assembled pizza to the heated pizza stone. Prick the pizza base all over with a fork.

Spread the pizza sauce evenly over the pizza base, and spread the garlic confit over the top. Scatter over the shredded mozzarella, buffalo mozzarella, and parsley. Place the tomato and pepperoni slices around the pizza evenly and season with salt and pepper.

Transfer the pizza onto the preheated pizza stone. Cook the pizza in the oven for 5-10 minutes or until golden and crisp. Carefully remove the pizza from the oven using a pizza peel or wide spatula and transfer to a cutting board. Scatter over the mint leaves, if using, and extra buffalo mozzarella pieces. Sprinkle with dried chile flakes, if desired, and serve.

Semolina or all-purpose flour, for rolling

6 oz pizza dough (see p 15)

⅓ cup pizza sauce (see p 19)

1 garlic confit clove (see p 20), crushed

½ cup shredded mozzarella

1 oz buffalo mozzarella, torn, + ½ oz extra, torn into small pieces

1 tablespoon chopped fresh flat-leaf (Italian) parsley

1 roma tomato, sliced thinly into 8 slices

12 slices large pepperoni or 30 slices small pepperoni

Sea salt and freshly ground black pepper

12 large mint leaves, optional

Pinch of dried chile flakes, optional

MAKES ONE 12-INCH ROUND PIZZA

SERVES 1–2

Mushroom, Ham, and Ricotta Cheese

The addition of ricotta cheese to any pizza brings an element of lightness and really lets the other ingredients shine. Reducing the balsamic vinegar gives the vinegar some sweetness, which works great with the ham, ricotta, and mushrooms. I wouldn't say this is a knock-your-socks-off type of pizza with bold flavors, but is more the type of pizza that everyone will enjoy from children to grown ups, and fussy eaters in between. If you wanted to inject a bit more "fun" into this pizza, you could replace the ricotta cheese with some fontina, and hold on!

1 large mushroom, such as Portobello

1 tablespoon olive oil

Semolina or all-purpose flour, for rolling

6 oz pizza dough (see p 15)

1/3 cup pizza sauce (see p 19)

1 tablespoon oregano leaves, + extra leaves to serve

1 tablespoon garlic confit (see p 20), crushed

1/2 cup shredded mozzarella

1 1/2 oz fresh ricotta cheese, crumbled

3 oz ham, thinly sliced

Sea salt and freshly ground black pepper

Balsamic reduction (see p 18), to serve

MAKES ONE 12-INCH ROUND PIZZA

SERVES 1–2

Place a pizza stone in the oven. Preheat the oven to 350°F (180°C). Place the mushroom on a small baking tray, drizzle with the olive oil, and roast for 8 minutes or until tender, then slice.

Increase the oven temperature to 500°F (260°C) or to its highest temperature. Once it has reached the temperature, it will then take about 15 minutes for the pizza stone to heat up.

Lightly dust a clean work surface with semolina or flour, then roll out the dough into a 12-inch round that is 1/8 inch thick. Transfer the pizza base onto a piece of parchment paper; this is necessary for transferring the assembled pizza to the heated pizza stone. Prick the pizza base all over with a fork.

Spread the pizza base evenly with the pizza sauce, then top with the oregano, garlic confit, mozzarella, ricotta cheese, sliced mushroom, and ham. Season with salt and pepper.

Transfer the pizza onto the preheated pizza stone. Cook the pizza in the oven for 5-10 minutes or until golden and crisp. Carefully remove the pizza from the oven using a pizza peel or wide spatula and transfer to a cutting board. Scatter with the extra oregano leaves and serve with a drizzle of balsamic reduction.

GORGONZOLA WITH FIG AND PANCETTA

When the first figs of the season appear, this pizza goes straight onto the specials board at my restaurant. There is something so uniquely Italian about the combination of gorgonzola, pancetta or prosciutto, and figs together. One of my favorite dishes is to take ripe figs and slice them across the top into four, stuff them with gorgonzola and wrap them in prosciutto, then roast them in the oven with a touch of cream, until they are soft, gooey, and lusciously rich. This follows the same idea. You can freshen it up by topping the pizza with a simple dressed arugula salad, or just leave it as is.

Place a pizza stone in the oven and preheat the oven to 500°F (260°C) or to its highest temperature. Once it has reached the temperature, it will then take about 15 minutes for the pizza stone to heat up.

Lightly dust a clean work surface with semolina or flour, then roll out the dough into a rough 4 × 10-inch oval about ⅛ inch thick. Transfer the pizza base onto a piece of parchment paper; this is necessary for transferring the assembled pizza to the heated pizza stone. Prick the pizza base all over with a fork.

Brush the pizza base with the olive oil. Place the torn basil leaves on top of the pizza base, followed by the tomato slices. Sprinkle over the shredded mozzarella and crumble over the gorgonzola. Lay the thin slices of pancetta on top and season with salt and pepper.

Transfer the pizza onto the preheated pizza stone. Cook the pizza in the oven for 5-10 minutes or until golden and crisp. Carefully remove the pizza from the oven using a pizza peel or wide spatula and transfer to a cutting board.

Arrange the figs on the pizza, scatter with wild arugula, then drizzle with the balsamic reduction. Season with salt and pepper to taste, and serve.

Semolina or all-purpose flour, for rolling

6 oz pizza dough (see p 15)

1 tablespoon olive oil

12 large fresh basil leaves, torn

2 ripe roma tomatoes, thinly sliced

½ cup shredded mozzarella

2 oz gorgonzola

8 very thin slices pancetta

Sea salt and freshly ground black pepper

2 small fresh figs, each torn into 4 wedges

Wild arugula, to serve

1 tablespoon balsamic reduction (see p 18), or apple balsamic vinegar

MAKES ONE 4 X 10-INCH OVAL PIZZA

SERVES 1–2

Italian Sausage with Sweet-and-Sour Bell Peppers

Italians have a wonderful relationship with the pig, as you can see from all the delicious meats they produce such as prosciutto, pancetta, cotechino, salami, pepperoni, coppa, and Parma ham. They also make some of the best sausages in the world, especially the pork and fennel, which is my favorite. If you have the time, make my Spicy Italian Sausage Mix (see p 21) or, next time you are at the butcher and you see some Italian-style sausages, grab a couple as sausage meat makes a great topping for a pizza.

4 oz baby spinach

Semolina or all-purpose flour, for rolling

6 oz pizza dough (see p 15)

⅓ cup pizza sauce (see p 19)

1 tablespoon chopped fresh flat-leaf (Italian) parsley

4 oz spicy Italian sausage mix (see p 21)

1½ oz taleggio cheese, cut into small cubes

½ cup shredded mozzarella

Sea salt and freshly ground black pepper

¾ cup peperonata (see p 20)

Small handful of wild arugula

MAKES ONE 6 X 10-INCH OVAL PIZZA

SERVES 1

Cook the spinach in boiling salted water until just wilted. Refresh in iced water, drain, and squeeze out the water.

Place a pizza stone in the oven and preheat the oven to 500°F (260°C) or to its highest temperature. Once it has reached the temperature, it will then take about 15 minutes for the pizza stone to heat up.

Lightly dust a clean work surface with semolina or flour, then roll out the dough into a rough 6 × 10-inch oval that is ⅛ inch thick. Transfer the pizza base onto a piece of parchment paper; this is necessary for transferring the assembled pizza to the heated pizza stone. Prick the pizza base all over with a fork.

Spread the pizza sauce evenly over the pizza base and scatter with the chopped parsley.

Divide the sausage mix into 16 roughly rolled balls. Scatter the pizza base with the blanched spinach, spicy sausage balls, and taleggio, then sprinkle with the mozzarella. Season with salt and pepper.

Transfer the pizza onto the preheated pizza stone. Cook the pizza in the oven for 5-10 minutes or until golden and crisp. Carefully remove the pizza from the oven using a pizza peel or wide spatula and transfer to a cutting board.

Scatter the peperonata and arugula over the top. Season with salt and pepper and serve.

Zucchini with Mozzarella and Leek

You have to love a pizza that only has a few ingredients, but looks so good when it gets to the table. This pizza takes the humblest of vegetables, the zucchini, and makes it the hero. If only all things in life could be this simple. If you can't get a hold of zucchini flowers, slice a zucchini, broil it briefly with olive oil to soften it, and use it in exactly the same way.

Melt the butter in a small saucepan over medium heat. Once the butter has melted, add the chopped leek and cook, stirring occasionally, for 5-8 minutes or until softened. Season to taste with salt and pepper. Set aside.

Place a pizza stone in the oven and preheat the oven to 500°F (260°C) or to its highest temperature. Once it has reached the temperature, it will then take about 15 minutes for the pizza stone to heat up.

Lightly dust a clean work surface with semolina or flour, then roll out the dough into a 12-inch round that is ⅛ inch thick. Transfer the pizza base onto a piece of parchment paper; this is necessary for transferring the assembled pizza to the heated pizza stone. Prick the pizza base all over with a fork.

Heat half the garlic oil in a large skillet over high heat, season the zucchini with salt and pepper, and fry in batches for 1-2 minutes or until they have slightly caramelized on one side. Set aside. Repeat with the remaining oil and zucchini.

Mix the pizza sauce, goat cheese, ricotta, and garlic confit together in a bowl, then spread evenly over the pizza base. Season with salt and pepper. Scatter over the shredded mozzarella, cooked leek, chile flakes, if using, and torn parsley. Arrange the zucchini around the pizza, along with the zucchini flowers and buffalo mozzarella.

Transfer the pizza onto the preheated pizza stone. Cook the pizza in the oven for 5-10 minutes or until golden and crisp. Carefully remove the pizza from the oven using a pizza peel or wide spatula and transfer to a cutting board. Drizzle with a little lemon oil and finish with the extra torn parsley.

1 tablespoon butter

½ cup chopped leek, white part only

Sea salt and freshly ground black pepper

Semolina or all-purpose flour, for rolling

6 oz pizza dough (see p 15)

2 tablespoons garlic oil (use the oil from the garlic confit, see p 20), or vegetable oil

2 zucchini, thinly sliced

¼ cup pizza sauce (see p 19)

2 tablespoons goat cheese

1 tablespoon fresh ricotta cheese

1 garlic confit clove (see p 20), crushed

¼ cup shredded mozzarella

½-1 teaspoon dried chile flakes, optional

1 tablespoon torn flat-leaf (Italian) parsley, + extra to serve

6 zucchini flowers, flower part only and stamen removed

1½ oz buffalo mozzarella, torn

Drizzle of lemon oil

MAKES ONE 12-INCH ROUND PIZZA

SERVES 1–2

MODERN PIZZAS

CRAB WITH TOMATO AND AÏOLI

Crab on pizza is such an indulgence, and delicious, too. The squeeze of lemon juice just before serving turns this pizza into something fantastic—it lifts the flavor of the entire pizza, complementing the richness of the aïoli, and it is an imperative part of the recipe. Alaskan king crab, or any top quality cooked crab meat, is perfect for this recipe. Make sure you leave it in large chunks when you top the pizza. If using pre-picked crab meat, gently squeeze any excess liquid from it.

5 oz cooked crab meat, picked

1 teaspoon fresh flat-leaf (Italian) parsley, chopped, + 1 tablespoon extra

1 tablespoon lemon zest

2 tablespoons lemon oil

1½ tablespoons garlic confit (see p 20), crushed

Sea salt and freshly ground black pepper

Semolina or all-purpose flour, for rolling

6 oz pizza dough (see p 15)

⅓ cup pizza sauce (see p 19)

½ cup shredded mozzarella

1 tomato, cut into ⅛-inch-thick slices

2 tablespoons aïoli (see p 18)

Squeeze of lemon, to serve

1 fresh long red chile, such as Anaheim or New Mexico, cut into julienne

MAKES ONE 8 X 12-INCH RECTANGLE PIZZA

SERVES 1–2

Place the crab meat in a bowl, add the chopped parsley, lemon zest, lemon oil, and ½ tablespoon garlic confit. Season with salt and pepper. Set aside for 10 minutes to marinate.

Place a pizza stone in the oven and preheat the oven to 500°F (260°C) or to its highest temperature. Once it has reached the temperature, it will then take about 15 minutes for the pizza stone to heat up.

Lightly dust a clean work surface with semolina or flour, then roll out the dough into a rough 8 × 12-inch rectangle that is about ⅛ inch thick. Transfer the pizza base onto a piece of parchment paper; this is necessary for transferring the assembled pizza to the heated pizza stone. Prick the pizza base all over with a fork.

Spread the pizza sauce evenly over the pizza base. Sprinkle with the shredded mozzarella, some of the extra chopped parsley, remaining garlic confit, and sliced tomato. Arrange the marinated crab on the pizza and season with salt and pepper.

Transfer the pizza onto the preheated pizza stone. Cook the pizza in the oven for 5-10 minutes or until golden and crisp.

Meanwhile, combine the aïoli with 1 teaspoon of water in a small bowl.

Carefully remove the pizza from the oven using a pizza peel or wide spatula and transfer to a cutting board. Squeeze over some lemon juice and serve drizzled with the aïoli and scattered with the remaining chopped parsley and the chile.

BUTTERNUT SQUASH WITH GORGONZOLA AND PINE NUTS

If you have vegetarians coming for lunch or dinner and are perplexed about what to cook for them, look no further than this recipe. They will love it, and *you* for thinking of them. Gorgonzola is an Italian variety of blue-veined cheese but it is creamy and not as strong as other types of blue cheese. Adding roasted butternut squash, toasted pine nuts, and balsamic onions will ensure even the most hearty meat eater will love this pizza, too. Incidentally, when Rachael Ray came to Australia to film her TV series, this is the pizza I served her. I'm proud to say she loved it!

Place a pizza stone in the oven. Preheat the oven to 350°F (180°C). Place the butternut squash on a baking sheet, sprinkle with salt and pepper and drizzle with olive oil. Roast in the oven for about 12 minutes or until tender.

Increase the oven temperature to 500°F (260°C) or to its highest temperature. Once it has reached the temperature, it will then take about 15 minutes for the pizza stone to heat up.

Lightly dust a clean work surface with semolina or flour, then roll out the dough into a rough 12-inch square that is ⅛ inch thick. Transfer the pizza base onto parchment paper; this is necessary for transferring the assembled pizza to the heated pizza stone. Prick the pizza base all over with a fork.

Brush the pizza base evenly with the extra-virgin olive oil. Add the zucchini slices, crumbled gorgonzola, mozzarella, and roasted butternut squash, then sprinkle over the pine nuts, parsley, and balsamic onion, and season to taste with salt and pepper.

Transfer the pizza onto the preheated pizza stone. Cook the pizza in the oven for 5-10 minutes or until golden and crisp. While the pizza is cooking, heat the vegetable oil in a small saucepan over medium-high heat. Add the sage and cook for 30-60 seconds until crisp. Remove with a slotted spoon and drain on paper towels.

Carefully remove the pizza from the oven using a pizza peel or wide spatula and transfer to a cutting board. Sprinkle with the sage and serve.

4½ oz butternut squash, peeled and cut into ½-inch dice

Sea salt and freshly ground black pepper

1 tablespoon olive oil

Semolina or all-purpose flour, for rolling

6 oz pizza dough (see p 15)

1 tablespoon extra-virgin olive oil

½ large zucchini, sliced into ribbons

2 oz gorgonzola dolcelatte cheese

¼ cup shredded mozzarella

2 teaspoons pine nuts, lightly toasted

1 tablespoon chopped fresh flat-leaf (Italian) parsley

2 tablespoons balsamic onion (see p 19)

¼ cup vegetable oil

12 fresh sage leaves

MAKES ONE 12-INCH SQUARE PIZZA

SERVES 1–2

SHRIMP WITH SCALLOPS AND GREEN OLIVES

I could write a book on the virtues of eating seafood, but let's just say that it's very good for you, and the more you eat it, the healthier and happier you'll be. Play around with different sea creatures. In this recipe I've simply used shrimp with scallops, finished off perfectly with grated bottarga (cured and salted mullet or tuna caviar).

5 oz whole raw shrimp, peeled and deveined

6 small scallops, halved lengthwise

1 tablespoon garlic confit (see p 20), crushed

2 tablespoons chile confit (see p 19)

1 teaspoon lemon zest

1 tablespoon olive oil

Pinch of salt and freshly ground black pepper

Semolina or all-purpose flour, for rolling

6 oz pizza dough (see p 15)

⅓ cup pizza sauce (see p 19)

½ cup shredded mozzarella

1 tablespoon chopped fresh flat-leaf (Italian) parsley + extra 1 tablespoon leaves, to serve

⅓ cup cherry tomato salad (see p 31; replace the oregano with torn basil)

3 pitted Sicilian olives

Squeeze of lemon, to serve

Grated bottarga, optional

MAKES ONE 12-INCH ROUND PIZZA

SERVES 2

Place a pizza stone in the oven and preheat the oven to 500°F (260°C) or to its highest temperature. Once it has reached the temperature, it will then take about 15 minutes for the pizza stone to heat up.

Butterfly the shrimp and place in a bowl with the scallops. Add the garlic confit, chile confit, lemon zest, and olive oil and marinate for 10 minutes. Season with salt and pepper.

Lightly dust a clean work surface with semolina or flour, then roll out the dough into a 12-inch round that is ⅛ inch thick. Transfer the pizza base onto a piece of parchment paper; this is necessary for transferring the assembled pizza to the pizza stone. Prick the pizza base all over with a fork.

Spread the pizza sauce evenly over the pizza base. Sprinkle with the shredded mozzarella and the parsley. Arrange the marinated seafood over the top.

Transfer the pizza onto the preheated pizza stone. Cook the pizza in the oven for 5-10 minutes or until golden and crisp. Carefully remove the pizza from the oven using a pizza peel or wide spatula and transfer to a cutting board.

Sprinkle with the cherry tomato salad, olives, remaining parsley, a good squeeze of fresh lemon, and the grated bottarga, if using.

PUTTANESCA

There is a classic Italian dish called pasta puttanesca—there are a few stories as to where this pasta got its name, but the literal translation means "whore's pasta." The beauty of this pasta sauce is the combination of tomato, garlic, chile, capers, olives, and anchovies. All of these ingredients call out to be placed on top of a pizza along with some creamy buffalo mozzarella.

Place a pizza stone in the oven and preheat the oven to 500°F (260°C) or to its highest temperature. Once it has reached the temperature, it will then take about 15 minutes for the pizza stone to heat up.

Lightly dust a clean work surface with semolina or flour, then roll out the dough into a 12-inch round that is $\frac{1}{8}$ inch thick. Transfer the pizza base onto a piece of parchment paper; this is necessary for transferring the assembled pizza to the pizza stone. Prick the pizza base all over with a fork.

Spread the pizza sauce evenly over the pizza base. Scatter with the chopped parsley, shredded mozzarella, cherry tomatoes, capers, olives, garlic confit, and a pinch of chile flakes, if using. Season with salt and pepper.

Transfer the pizza onto the preheated pizza stone. Cook the pizza in the oven for 5-10 minutes or until golden and crisp. Carefully remove the pizza from the oven using a pizza peel or wide spatula and transfer to a cutting board. Scatter with the buffalo mozzarella, parsley leaves, and anchovies. Drizzle with some extra-virgin olive oil and serve.

Semolina or all-purpose flour, for rolling

6 oz pizza dough (see p 15)

$\frac{1}{3}$ cup pizza sauce (see p 19)

1 tablespoon chopped fresh flat-leaf (Italian) parsley, + extra 1 tablespoon leaves, to serve

$\frac{1}{2}$ cup shredded mozzarella

12 cherry tomatoes, cut in half

1 tablespoon baby capers, rinsed and drained

6 pitted Sicilian olives, cut in half

1 garlic confit clove (see p 20), crushed

Dried chile flakes, to taste, optional

Sea salt and freshly ground black pepper

2 oz buffalo mozzarella, torn into pieces

6 white anchovies

Extra-virgin olive oil, for drizzling

MAKES ONE 12-INCH ROUND PIZZA

SERVES 1–2

Pesto Chicken with Pine Nuts and Parmesan

Pesto is a beautiful sauce that is a great accompaniment to just about anything. Pesto originated in Genoa, Italy, and its name is from the Italian word "pestare" which means "to pound or to crush." This is a reference to the original method of preparation with a stone mortar and pestle.

2 tablespoons olive oil

4½ oz chicken breast, boneless

Semolina or all-purpose flour, for rolling

6 oz pizza dough (see p 15)

2 tablespoons onion confit (see p 20)

2 tablespoons garlic confit (see p 20), crushed

½ cup shredded mozzarella

1½ oz sun-dried tomatoes

Sea salt and freshly ground black pepper

1 tablespoon extra-virgin olive oil

2 tablespoons pesto (see p 18)

1 tablespoon pine nuts, lightly toasted

Shaved parmesan, to serve

Squeeze of lemon, to serve

MAKES ONE 6 X 10-INCH OVAL PIZZA

SERVES 1

Place a pizza stone in the oven and preheat the oven to 500°F (260°C) or to its highest temperature. Once it has reached the temperature, it will then take about 15 minutes for the pizza stone to heat up.

Heat half of the olive oil in a skillet over medium-high heat, add the chicken and cook for 1-2 minutes or until just seared. You don't want to cook it through as the chicken will continue to cook when the topped pizza is in the oven. Tear into rough pieces and set aside.

Lightly dust a clean work surface with semolina or flour, then roll out the dough into a rough 6 × 10-inch oval that is ⅛ inch thick. Transfer the pizza base onto a piece of parchment paper; this is necessary for transferring the assembled pizza to the heated pizza stone. Prick the pizza base all over with a fork.

Spread the remaining olive oil over the pizza base, then spread with the onion confit, followed by the garlic confit. Top with the seared chicken, then scatter with the shredded mozzarella and sun-dried tomatoes. Season with pepper and a little salt.

Transfer the pizza onto the preheated pizza stone. Cook the pizza in the oven for 5-10 minutes or until golden and crisp. Carefully remove the pizza from the oven using a pizza peel or wide spatula and transfer to a cutting board.

Combine the extra-virgin olive oil with the pesto. Garnish with the toasted pine nuts, shaved parmesan, and pesto. Serve with a squeeze of lemon.

Asparagus With Goat cheese, Egg, and Toasted Walnuts

This is a pizza I came up with after serving one of my favorite asparagus dishes in one of my restaurants. I would always serve steamed asparagus topped with a poached egg, nut brown butter sauce, and truffled pecorino. When I opened Hugo's Bar Pizza, I tried many different variations of this pizza until finally I had what I wanted. The feedback on this has been wonderful and it's fast become a favorite. When truffles are in season, shave generously!

Place a pizza stone in the oven and preheat the oven to 500°F (260°C) or to its highest temperature. Once it has reached the temperature, it will then take about 15 minutes for the pizza stone to heat up.

Lightly dust a clean work surface with semolina or flour, then roll out the dough into a rough 8 × 12-inch oval that is about ⅛ inch thick. Transfer the pizza base onto a piece of parchment paper; this is necessary for transferring the assembled pizza to the heated pizza stone. Prick the pizza base all over with a fork.

Brush the pizza base with the olive oil and spread the goat cheese evenly over the top. Spread with the garlic confit, then add the shredded mozzarella, onion confit, parsley, and asparagus, in that order. Season with salt and pepper.

Crack the egg into a cup. Transfer the pizza onto the preheated pizza stone, then add the egg to the center of the pizza and top with the grated parmesan. Season the egg with salt and pepper.

Cook the pizza in the oven for 5-10 minutes or until golden and crisp. Carefully remove the pizza from the oven using a pizza peel or wide spatula and transfer to a cutting board. Scatter over the shaved parmesan and walnuts, drizzle with the truffle oil or shave over some truffle and serve.

NOTE: If using an electric pizza oven, follow the instructions on page 11, adding the parmesan with the egg.

Semolina or all-purpose flour, for rolling

6 oz pizza dough (see p 15)

1 tablespoon olive oil

¼ cup fresh goat cheese

1 garlic confit clove (see p 20), crushed

½ cup shredded mozzarella

1½ tablespoons onion confit (see p 20)

1 tablespoon chopped flat-leaf (Italian) parsley

6 asparagus spears, blanched and halved lengthwise

Sea salt and freshly ground black pepper

1 free-range egg

1 tablespoon finely grated parmesan, + shaved parmesan, to serve

1 tablespoon toasted walnuts, crushed

1 teaspoon white truffle oil or fresh black truffle

MAKES ONE 8 X 12-INCH OVAL PIZZA

SERVES 1–2

SMOKED SALMON WITH CAVIAR AND MASCARPONE

If you don't want to spend hundreds of dollars going out to the finest restaurant in town, why not whip up this little number? It has smoked salmon which is cheaper than valet parking, and you can either splurge on the best caviar or go for simple salmon caviar, which won't break the bank but will give you a wonderful flavor and texture. And you can always get a table at home.

½ Spanish (red) onion

2 tablespoons olive oil, + extra 1 teaspoon, to serve

Semolina or all-purpose flour, for rolling

6 oz pizza dough (see p 15)

¼ cup pizza sauce (see p 19)

1 tablespoon chopped flat-leaf (Italian) parsley

½ cup shredded mozzarella

1 tablespoon capers, rinsed and dried on paper towels

4 oz smoked salmon slices (about 5 slices)

2 tablespoons mascarpone cheese

2 tablespoons avruga caviar or salmon caviar

LEMON DRESSING

1 tablespoon lemon juice

1 tablespoon olive oil

Pinch of sea salt and freshly ground black pepper

Handful of fresh watercress

MAKES ONE 12-INCH ROUND PIZZA

SERVES 1–2

Place a pizza stone in the oven. Preheat the oven to 350°F (180°C). Cut the onion into ⅛-inch-thick slices and toss in 1 tablespoon of the oil. Place the onion slices on a parchment paper-lined baking sheet in a single layer. Roast for 4 minutes or until the onion is soft.

Increase oven to 500°F (260°C) or to its highest temperature. Once it has reached the temperature, it will then take about 15 minutes for the pizza stone to heat up.

Lightly dust a clean work surface with semolina or flour, then roll out the dough into a 12-inch round that is ⅛ inch thick. Transfer the pizza base onto a piece of parchment paper; this is necessary for transferring the assembled pizza to the pizza stone. Prick the pizza base all over with a fork.

Spread the pizza sauce evenly over the base. Sprinkle with the chopped parsley and shredded mozzarella. Top with the onion. Transfer the pizza onto the preheated pizza stone. Cook the pizza in the oven for 5-10 minutes or until golden and crisp.

Meanwhile, heat 1 tablespoon olive oil in a very small skillet over medium-high heat and fry the capers until crisp. Drain on a paper towel. To make the lemon dressing, combine the lemon juice and oil in a bowl and season with salt and pepper. Add the watercress and toss to combine.

Carefully remove the pizza from the oven using a pizza peel or wide spatula and transfer to a cutting board. Top with slices of salmon, the lemon dressing, and dollops of mascarpone topped with caviar. Sprinkle with the crisp capers. Drizzle with the remaining 1 teaspoon olive oil and finish with a grind of black pepper.

Bresaola with Baby Beets, Tomato Chutney, and Horseradish

My good friends and right handers in the kitchen, Monica Cannataci and her twin sister Jacinta, have been working with me for the past eight years. Monica recently won first place in a national pizza competition with this pizza. Bresaola is Italian air-dried beef, served in paper-thin slices. It's available from delicatessens. You could also use thinly sliced roast beef or smoked salmon.

Place a pizza stone in the oven. Preheat the oven to 350°F (180°C). Place the beets on a piece of foil, drizzle with olive oil, and fold to seal. Place on a baking sheet and roast for 45 minutes or until the beets are tender. Cool slightly, then peel and cut into wedges.

Increase the oven temperature to 500°F (260°C) or to its highest temperature. Once it has reached the temperature, it will then take about 15 minutes for the pizza stone to heat up.

Lightly dust a clean work surface with semolina or flour, then roll out the dough into a 12-inch round that is ⅛ inch thick. Transfer the pizza base onto a piece of parchment paper; this is necessary for transferring the assembled pizza to the pizza stone. Prick the pizza base all over with a fork.

Combine the goat cheese and sour cream together in a bowl, then evenly spread over the pizza base. Scatter over the parsley, then add the garlic and onion confit, tomato chutney, and mozzarella, in that order. Season with salt and pepper.

Transfer the pizza onto the preheated pizza stone. Cook the pizza in the oven for 5-10 minutes or until golden and crisp. Carefully remove the pizza from the oven using a pizza peel or wide spatula and transfer to a cutting board.

Fan the bresaola neatly on the hot pizza, then scatter with the beets, and a small amount of finely grated horseradish. Serve topped with the watercress, lemon oil, apple balsamic, and shaved pecorino. Sprinkle with sea salt.

3 baby beets

1 tablespoon olive oil

Semolina or all-purpose flour, for rolling

6 oz pizza dough (see p 15)

1½ tablespoons goat cheese

1½ tablespoons sour cream

1 tablespoon fresh flat-leaf (Italian) parsley, chopped

1 tablespoon garlic confit (see p 20), crushed

1 tablespoon onion confit (see p 20)

2 tablespoons tomato chutney (see p 21) or good-quality store bought

½ cup shredded mozzarella

Sea salt and freshly ground black pepper

15 very thin slices bresaola

1-inch piece fresh horseradish, peeled

Small handful of picked watercress sprigs

1 teaspoon lemon oil

1 teaspoon apple balsamic or balsamic reduction (see p 18)

Shaved truffled pecorino, to serve

MAKES ONE 12-INCH ROUND PIZZA

SERVES 1–2

TUNA WITH GREEN OLIVE SALSA

This pizza takes its inspiration from Sicily with green olives and the tuna that swims along the coast there. Substitute fresh for canned if you've got it—either put on very thin raw slices or slowly cook it, submerged in olive oil, at 113°F (45°C) until just falling apart.

Semolina or all-purpose flour, for rolling

6 oz pizza dough (see p 15)

⅓ cup pizza sauce (see p 19)

1 tablespoon chopped fresh flat-leaf (Italian) parsley

½ cup shredded mozzarella

¼ Spanish (red) onion, thinly sliced

1 tablespoon baby capers, rinsed

3 oz canned tuna in oil, drained and flaked

Sea salt and freshly ground black pepper

Drizzle of olive oil, to serve

Small handful of watercress leaves

GREEN OLIVE SALSA

½ cup green olives, pitted, halved, and sliced

2 tablespoons finely diced fennel

1 tablespoon chopped fresh flat-leaf (Italian) parsley

2 tablespoons lemon-infused olive oil

¼ cup sun-dried tomatoes, diced

Sea salt and freshly ground black pepper

MAKES ONE 12-INCH ROUND PIZZA

SERVES 1–2

Place a pizza stone in the oven and preheat the oven to 500°F (260°C) or to its highest temperature. Once it has reached the temperature, it will then take about 15 minutes for the pizza stone to heat up.

Lightly dust a clean work surface with semolina or flour, then roll out the dough into a 12-inch round that is ⅛ inch thick. Transfer the pizza base onto a piece of parchment paper; this is necessary for transferring the assembled pizza to the pizza stone. Prick the pizza base all over with a fork.

Spread the pizza sauce evenly over the pizza base. Sprinkle over the chopped parsley and the mozzarella. Scatter over the Spanish onion, capers, and tuna. Season with salt and freshly ground black pepper. (Be mindful that the capers and olives are quite salty.)

Transfer the pizza onto the preheated pizza stone. Cook the pizza in the oven for 5-10 minutes or until golden and crisp.

While the pizza is cooking, combine the salsa ingredients in a bowl and season with salt and pepper.

Carefully remove the pizza from the oven using a pizza peel or wide spatula and transfer to a cutting board.

Spoon the salsa over the pizza, drizzle with olive oil, and arrange the watercress over the top. Serve.

CARBONARA

One of the first pasta dishes I learned to cook was spaghetti carbonara. I was amazed at how simple it was to make, but more importantly how much flavor it packed from using only a few ingredients well. The heroes are, of course, the egg, cheese, and pancetta, or bacon. For the pizza, I have just added some buffalo mozzarella to the base so that the egg, pancetta, and parmesan can shine. Serve with lots of black pepper.

Place a pizza stone in the oven and preheat the oven to 500°F (260°C) or to its highest temperature. Once it has reached the temperature, it will then take about 15 minutes for the pizza stone to heat up.

Lightly dust a clean work surface with semolina or flour, then roll out the dough into a rough 8 × 12-inch oval that is about ⅛ inch thick. Transfer the pizza base onto a piece of parchment paper; this is necessary for transferring the assembled pizza to the heated pizza stone. Prick the pizza base all over with a fork.

Brush the pizza base with oil, then scatter with the shredded mozzarella, onion confit, parsley, and torn buffalo mozzarella. Lay the pancetta over the top and season with salt and lots of freshly ground black pepper.

Crack the eggs into separate cups. Transfer the pizza onto the pizza stone, add the eggs to the pizza and top with the grated parmesan. Season the eggs with freshly ground black pepper.

Cook the pizza in the oven for 5-10 minutes or until golden and crisp. Carefully remove the pizza from the oven using a pizza peel or wide spatula and transfer to a cutting board. Serve sprinkled with extra parsley, the Parmigiano Reggiano, and plenty of freshly ground black pepper.

NOTE: If using an electric pizza oven, follow the instructions on page 11, adding the parmesan with the egg.

Semolina or all-purpose flour, for rolling

6 oz pizza dough (see p 15)

1 tablespoon olive oil

½ cup shredded mozzarella

2 tablespoons onion confit (see p 20)

1 tablespoon chopped fresh flat-leaf (Italian) parsley, + 1 extra tablespoon, to serve

1½ oz buffalo mozzarella, torn into pieces

8 very thin slices pancetta

Sea salt and freshly ground black pepper

3 free-range eggs

2 tablespoons finely grated parmesan

Shaved Parmigiano Reggiano, to serve

MAKES ONE 8 X 12-INCH OVAL PIZZA

SERVES 1–2

CHILE SHRIMP WITH ROASTED BELL PEPPER AND SALSA VERDE

When you make pizzas at home, you should think about what you put on your pizza before it goes into your oven, as well as what you can put on after it comes out. One of the classic pizzas is Prosciutto with Arugula and Parmesan (see p 40). The beauty of that pizza is the ingredients that are added after it is cooked such as the prosciutto, parmesan, and arugula. So too with this pizza: the chile shrimp are delicious when teamed with the roasted bell pepper and tomato, but once it comes out of the oven, pop on the salsa verde (Italian for green sauce). It isn't necessary with every pizza to top it once it comes out of the oven, but play around, as you can have a lot of fun with it, from different salad leaves, herbs, cheeses, nuts, and spices.

Semolina or all-purpose flour, for rolling

6 oz pizza dough (see p 15)

¼ cup pizza sauce (see p 19)

1 tablespoon fresh flat-leaf (Italian) parsley, chopped

10 cherry tomatoes, each cut into 3 slices

½ cup shredded mozzarella

1 oz roasted red bell pepper (see p 20 or good-quality store bought), cut into strips

3½ oz jumbo shrimp, peeled and butterflied

1½ oz buffalo mozzarella, torn

Sea salt and freshly ground black pepper

Pinch of dried chile flakes, optional

1½ tablespoons salsa verde (see p 19)

MAKES ONE 12-INCH ROUND PIZZA

SERVES 1–2

Place a pizza stone in the oven and preheat the oven to 500°F (260°C) or to its highest temperature. Once it has reached the temperature, it will then take about 15 minutes for the pizza stone to heat up.

Lightly dust a clean work surface with semolina or flour, then roll out the dough into a 12-inch round that is ⅛ inch thick. Transfer the pizza base onto a piece of parchment paper; this is necessary for transferring the assembled pizza to the heated pizza stone. Prick the pizza base all over with a fork.

Spread the pizza sauce evenly over the pizza base. Sprinkle with the parsley, cherry tomatoes, and shredded mozzarella. Arrange the bell pepper and shrimp over the top, followed by the buffalo mozzarella. Sprinkle with sea salt, freshly ground black pepper, and dried chile flakes, if desired.

Transfer the pizza onto the preheated pizza stone. Cook the pizza in the oven for 5-10 minutes or until golden and crisp. Carefully remove the pizza from the oven using a pizza peel or wide spatula and transfer to a cutting board. Serve drizzled with the salsa verde.

Gorgonzola with Walnuts, Truffle Honey, and Radicchio

Gorgonzola makes my top five favorite cheeses. When entertaining guests during the cooler months of the year, I get a large piece of gorgonzola and place it in a heatproof dish, warm it until it just starts to melt, then drizzle it with truffle honey. I serve it with toasted sourdough bread to help scoop up the runny cheese and honey. I have adapted this way of serving cheese into this wonderful pizza to be more of a meal than a dessert.

Place two pizza stones in the oven and preheat the oven to 500°F (260°C) or to its highest temperature. Once it has reached the temperature, it will then take about 15 minutes for the pizza stones to heat up.

Lightly dust a clean work surface with semolina or flour, then roll out the dough into two 6-inch rounds that are ⅛ inch thick. Transfer the pizza bases onto squares of parchment paper; this is necessary for transferring the assembled pizzas to the heated pizza stones. Prick the pizza bases all over with a fork.

Brush each pizza with ½ tablespoon of the olive oil and sprinkle with the parsley. Crumble the gorgonzola and the shredded mozzarella over the top. Season with freshly ground black pepper.

Transfer the pizzas onto the preheated pizza stones. Cook the pizzas in the oven for 5-10 minutes or until golden and crisp.

Meanwhile, heat a small skillet with the remaining olive oil over medium heat, add the radicchio, and cook for 1 minute or until the radicchio is just wilted. Season with a little salt. Set aside.

Carefully remove the pizzas from the oven using a pizza peel or wide spatula and transfer to a cutting board. Arrange the radicchio leaves on top of the pizzas. Drizzle with the truffle honey and serve sprinkled with the walnuts.

Semolina or all-purpose flour, for rolling

2 × 3-oz pizza doughs (see p 15)

1½ tablespoons olive oil

1 tablespoon chopped fresh flat-leaf (Italian) parsley

2½ oz gorgonzola cheese, crumbled

½ cup shredded mozzarella

Sea salt and freshly ground black pepper

3 radicchio leaves, washed and torn in half

1 tablespoon truffle honey

½ cup walnuts, toasted and coarsely chopped

MAKES TWO 6-INCH ROUND PIZZAS

SERVES 1–2

Croque Monsieur

Traveling through France, you fall in love with so many things: the beauty of the countryside, the wonderful accent, the wine, the women (or men...) and, of course, the food. France is known as being a birthplace for great food in the world and rightly so; they have produced not only some of the best chefs and restaurants but also some of the most wonderful recipes that have stood the test of time. Croque monsieur is a simple little toasted ham and cheese sandwich that is flavored with mustard. I have redesigned it to become a wonderful breakfast pizza. You can also add some cooked spinach or a poached or fried egg to it if you like.

Semolina or all-purpose flour, for rolling

2 × 2½-oz pizza doughs (see p 15)

Olive oil, for brushing

1 tablespoon dijon mustard

4 fresh basil leaves, torn

¼ cup shredded mozzarella

1½ oz buffalo mozzarella, torn into pieces

2½ oz smoked leg ham, shaved

2 oz gruyère cheese, shaved

Sea salt and freshly ground black pepper

4 small cornichons (baby pickles), sliced

MAKES ONE 6-INCH PIZZA SANDWICH

SERVES 1–2

Place two pizza stones in the oven and preheat the oven to 500°F (260°C) or to its highest temperature. Once it has reached the temperature, it will then take about 15 minutes for the pizza stones to heat up.

Lightly dust a clean work surface with semolina or flour, and then roll out each dough into two 6-inch rounds that are about ⅛ inch thick. Transfer the pizza bases onto pieces of parchment paper. This is necessary for transferring the assembled pizzas to the pizza stones. Prick the pizza bases all over with a fork.

Brush some olive oil evenly over the pizzas, then smear with the mustard. Scatter over the torn basil leaves, shredded mozzarella, buffalo mozzarella, ham, and gruyère. Season with salt and pepper. Transfer the pizzas onto the preheated pizza stones and cook for 5-10 minutes or until golden and crisp.

Carefully remove the pizzas from the oven using a pizza peel or wide spatula and transfer to a cutting board. Top one of the pizzas with the cornichons, then carefully flip the remaining pizza, topping side down, onto the first pizza (all the cheese should be on the inside). Return to the pizza stone in the oven for a couple of minutes before serving.

NOTE: This recipe cannot be adapted for an electric pizza oven.

THE BLT

What could be more delicious than a BLT? A BLT pizza, that's what! I like to play around with the ingredients on this pizza by using different types of pork products for the bacon such as pancetta, prosciutto, salami, and speck as well as different types of lettuce, like iceberg, romaine, chicory, endive, treviso, or radicchio, and lastly trying cherry tomatoes, heirloom tomatoes, fried green tomatoes, truss tomatoes, and, if you're in the mood, replace the mayonnaise for aïoli (see p 18). I also make this at home as a BLAT which has the addition of beautiful ripe avocado (add after cooking) to freshen the pizza up and make it really irresistible.

Place a pizza stone in the oven and preheat the oven to 500°F (260°C) or to its highest temperature. Once it has reached the temperature, it will then take about 15 minutes for the pizza stone to heat up.

Lightly dust a clean work surface with semolina or flour, then roll out the dough into a rough 4 × 10-inch oval that is about ⅛ inch thick. Transfer the pizza base onto a piece of parchment paper; this is necessary for transferring the assembled pizza to the heated pizza stone. Prick the pizza base all over with a fork.

Spread the pizza sauce evenly over the pizza base, then scatter over the chopped parsley and shredded mozzarella. Arrange the tomato slices on the pizza. Scatter on the bacon, then season with salt and pepper.

Transfer the pizza onto the preheated pizza stone. Cook the pizza in the oven for 5-10 minutes or until golden and crisp. Carefully remove the pizza from the oven using a pizza peel or wide spatula and transfer to a cutting board.

Arrange the lettuce leaves on top of the cooked pizza and drizzle with the mayonnaise or aïoli. Serve.

Semolina or all-purpose flour, for rolling

6 oz pizza dough (see p 15)

⅓ cup pizza sauce (see p 19)

1 tablespoon chopped fresh flat-leaf (Italian) parsley

½ cup shredded mozzarella

1 ripe roma tomato, cut into ⅛ inch slices

3 strips bacon, rind removed, torn into pieces

Sea salt and freshly ground black pepper

4 baby romaine lettuce leaves, torn

2 tablespoons mayonnaise or aïoli (see p 18)

MAKES ONE 4 X 10-INCH OVAL PIZZA

SERVES 1–2

SMOKY BARBECUE CHICKEN

I know chicken's not strictly a traditional pizza topping, but it tastes unreal when it's done properly, so that's why I have included it here. If you have any leftover roast or barbecue chicken, use that instead of breasts. No need to panfry it, just slice and add plenty of barbecue sauce so that it doesn't dry out.

4½ oz chicken breast, skin on

Sea salt and freshly ground black pepper

1 tablespoon olive oil

Semolina or all-purpose flour, for rolling

6 oz pizza dough (see p 15)

3 tablespoons smoky barbecue sauce, + extra to serve

1 tablespoon chopped flat-leaf (Italian) parsley

1½ oz shredded mozzarella

½ roasted red bell pepper, (see p 20 or good-quality store bought), diced

¼ cup balsamic onion (see p 19)

1½ oz smoked mozzarella (scarmoza), torn into small pieces

Small handful of fresh cilantro leaves

Dried chile flakes, to serve, optional

MAKES ONE 8 X 12-INCH RECTANGLE PIZZA

SERVES 1–2

Place a pizza stone in the oven. Preheat the oven to 400°F (200°C). Season the chicken with salt and freshly ground black pepper, drizzle with oil, and cook in a skillet over a medium-high heat. Sear for 2 minutes on each side just to seal. Transfer to a baking dish and roast in the oven for 7-10 minutes until cooked through. Set aside to rest for 10-15 minutes. When cool, cut into ⅛-inch slices.

Increase the oven temperature to 500°F (260°C) or to its highest temperature. Once it has reached the temperature, it will then take about 15 minutes for the pizza stone to heat up.

Lightly dust a clean work surface with semolina or flour, then roll out the dough into a 8 × 12-inch rectangle that is about ⅛ inch thick. Transfer the pizza base onto a piece of parchment paper; this is necessary for transferring the assembled pizza to the heated pizza stone. Prick the pizza base all over with a fork.

Spread the barbecue sauce evenly over the pizza base and sprinkle with the chopped parsley and shredded mozzarella. Add the bell pepper, onion, chicken, and smoked mozzarella. Season with pepper and a little salt.

Transfer the pizza onto the preheated pizza stone. Cook the pizza in the oven for 5-10 minutes or until golden and crisp. Carefully remove the pizza from the oven using a pizza peel or wide spatula and transfer to a cutting board. Serve with a drizzle of barbecue sauce, the cilantro leaves, and dried chile flakes, if using, sprinkled over the top.

PANZANELLA

There are two ways to serve this. One is to reinvent the salad as a topping, or you can cook up some pizza dough and break it into a bowl with all the ingredients for a delicious summer salad.

Place a pizza stone in the oven. To make the oven-roasted tomatoes, preheat the oven to 280°F (138°C). Place the tomato halves on a rimmed baking sheet and sprinkle with oregano, salt and pepper, and then drizzle with olive oil. Roast in the oven for 15 minutes or until softened. Set aside and allow to cool.

To make the toasted breadcrumbs, increase the oven temperature to 350°F (180°C). Mix the garlic and olive oil with the breadcrumbs and spread out onto a baking sheet. Roast for 6 minutes or until golden.

Increase the oven temperature to 500°F (260°C) or to its highest temperature. Once it has reached the temperature, it will then take about 15 minutes for the pizza stone to heat up.

Lightly dust a clean work surface with semolina or flour, then roll out the dough into a rough 8 × 12-inch rectangle that is ⅛ inch thick. Transfer the pizza base onto a piece of parchment paper; this is necessary for transferring the assembled pizza to the heated pizza stone. Prick the pizza base all over with a fork.

Spread the pizza sauce evenly over the pizza base and sprinkle with the chopped parsley and mozzarella. Scatter over the olives and bell pepper strips, and season with salt and pepper.

Transfer the pizza onto the preheated pizza stone. Cook in the oven for 5-10 minutes or until golden and crisp. Carefully remove the pizza from the oven using a pizza peel or wide spatula and transfer to a cutting board.

Meanwhile, to make the dressing, mix the sherry vinegar and olive oil together in a bowl. Toss in the parsley, oven-roasted tomatoes, and the anchovies (if using), and season with salt and pepper.

Arrange the oven-roasted tomato salad on top of the pizza, along with the cucumber ribbons. Serve sprinkled with the feta and breadcrumbs.

Semolina or all-purpose flour, for dusting

6 oz pizza dough (see p 15)

⅓ cup pizza sauce (see p 19)

1 tablespoon fresh flat-leaf (Italian) parsley, chopped

½ cup shredded mozzarella

8 kalamata olives, pitted

1 roasted bell pepper (see p 20, or good-quality store bought), cut into strips

1 small cucumber, peeled into thin ribbons, seeds removed

1½ oz feta, crumbled

OVEN-ROASTED TOMATOES

10 cherry tomatoes, cut in half

1 teaspoon dried oregano

Sea salt and freshly ground black pepper

1 tablespoon olive oil

TOASTED BREADCRUMBS

2 garlic cloves, chopped

2 tablespoons extra-virgin olive oil

1 slice sourdough bread with crust on, torn into small pieces

DRESSING

2 teaspoons sherry vinegar

1 tablespoon extra-virgin olive oil

¼ cup fresh flat-leaf (Italian) parsley leaves

3 white anchovies, torn, optional

MAKES ONE 8 X 12-INCH RECTANGLE PIZZA

SERVES 1–2

SPECIAL PIZZAS

LAMB SHANK CALZONE

When creating a calzone, you have to use a filling that is wetter than what you would normally pop on a pizza. This luscious ragu becomes the best filling in the world.

1 tablespoon olive oil

1 lamb shank, trimmed of excess fat

½ onion, diced

1 garlic clove, crushed

½ stalk celery, finely diced

½ small carrot, finely diced

½ red bell pepper, seeds removed and diced

1 teaspoon fresh thyme leaves, chopped

1 tablespoon tomato paste

¼ cup red wine

14-oz can diced tomatoes

¼ cup fresh or frozen green peas

6 cups chicken or vegetable broth

½ cup canned white cannellini beans, rinsed and drained

Sea salt and freshly ground black pepper

Semolina or all-purpose flour, for rolling

5 × 3-oz pizza doughs (see p 15)

MAKES FIVE 6-INCH CALZONI

SERVES 5

Place 2 pizza stones in the oven. Preheat the oven to 325°F (165°C). Put a flameproof medium-sized casserole pot (that has a fitted lid) over medium heat. Add half the oil and, when heated, add the shank and brown all over. Remove from the pan and set aside. Wipe the pan clean with paper towels. Return the pan to a medium-low heat. Add the remaining oil, then the onion and garlic and sweat for 3 minutes. Add the celery and carrot and sweat for 3 minutes, or until softened. Stir in the bell pepper and thyme, cook for 1 minute, add the tomato paste, and cook for 1 minute. Return the lamb to the pan with the wine, tomatoes, peas, and broth. Bring to a boil.

Remove the pot from the heat, put the lid on, and place in the oven. Cook for 1¾ hours, or until the lamb is falling off the bone. Lift out the lamb, cool slightly, and remove the meat from the bone. Discard the bone. Return the pan to medium-high heat and cook until the sauce reduces and thickens; this takes about 15-20 minutes. Stir in the beans, then return the lamb meat to the sauce and season to taste. Set aside to cool to room temperature.

Increase the oven temperature to 500°F (260°C) or to its highest setting. Once it has reached the temperature, it will then take about 15 minutes for the pizza stone to heat up.

Lightly dust a work surface with semolina or flour, then roll out each dough into a 6-inch round that is ⅛ inch thick. Transfer the pizza bases onto squares of parchment paper. This is necessary for transferring the assembled pizzas to the pizza stones. Prick the pizza bases all over with a fork.

Spoon ½ cup of the lamb ragu on one half of each pizza base, leaving a ¾ inch border. Fold the other side over the filling and pinch the edges together, pleating to prevent the mixture from escaping. Brush with oil and sprinkle with sea salt. Transfer two calzoni onto the pre-heated pizza stones. Cook for 8-10 minutes or until golden and crisp. Carefully remove the calzoni from the oven using a pizza peel or wide spatula and transfer to a cutting board. Repeat with the other calzoni. Serve.

Artichoke, Prosciutto, Spinach, and Mozzarella Calzone

This little recipe is a lovely one to make in minutes if you have pizza dough on hand—just open a jar of artichokes, drain off the brine or oil, then add some spinach, mozzarella, prosciutto or salami, and pizza sauce. Voila! You have a lovely weeknight meal with very little effort required.

Place two pizza stones in the oven and preheat the oven to 500°F (260°C) or to its highest setting. Once it has reached the temperature, it will then take about 15 minutes for the pizza stones to heat up.

Meanwhile, lightly dust a clean work surface with semolina or flour, and then roll out each of the doughs into a 6-inch round that is about ⅛ inch thick. Transfer the pizza bases onto squares of parchment paper; this is necessary for transferring the assembled pizzas to the pizza stone. Prick the pizza bases all over with a fork.

Spread the pizza sauce evenly over the pizza bases, then spread over the garlic confit. Layer the prosciutto, spinach, mozzarella, artichoke slices, and parsley over one half of each of the bases. Sprinkle with dried chile flakes and season with sea salt and freshly ground black pepper. Fold the other side over the filling and pinch the edges together, pleating to prevent the mixture from escaping. Brush with a little olive oil and sprinkle with some sea salt.

Transfer the calzoni onto the preheated pizza stones. Cook for 8-10 minutes or until golden and crisp. Carefully remove from the oven using a pizza peel or wide spatula and transfer to a cutting board. Serve.

Semolina or all-purpose flour, for rolling

2 × 3-oz pizza doughs (see p 15)

¼ cup pizza sauce (see p 19)

1 tablespoon garlic confit (see p 20), crushed

6 thin slices prosciutto

4 oz baby spinach, blanched, excess water squeezed out, seasoned

1½ oz jarred artichoke hearts, drained and cut into slices

3 oz buffalo mozzarella, sliced

⅓ cup torn fresh flat-leaf (Italian) parsley

Pinch of dried chile flakes

Sea salt and freshly ground black pepper

Olive oil, for brushing

MAKES TWO 6-INCH CALZONI

SERVES 2

MOM'S PASTA BOLOGNESE CALZONE

My mom was an adventurous cook, which is where my love of food comes from. She would cook Asian food before it was cool, and was quite handy at grilling a steak, but mom's real secret weapon in the kitchen was her spaghetti bolognese. The next day, if there were any leftovers, we would put it inside a couple of pieces of bread and stick it in the toasted sandwich maker to make the best toasted sandwich. And now, a calzone.

1 tablespoon olive oil

¼ onion, finely chopped

1 garlic clove, finely chopped

9 oz ground beef

¼ teaspoon dried oregano

¼ cup red wine (shiraz is good)

1 teaspoon tomato paste

1 teaspoon tomato ketchup

1 teaspoon sweet chile sauce or pinch of dried chile flakes

3 oz canned tomato soup

¼ cup chicken broth

Sea salt and freshly ground black pepper

1 tablespoon chopped fresh flat-leaf (Italian) parsley

3 oz dried macaroni, cooked

Semolina or all-purpose flour, for rolling

5 × 3-oz pizza doughs (see p 15)

¾ cup finely grated parmesan cheese, + extra 5 tablespoons

1 egg, beaten

MAKES FIVE 6-INCH CALZONI

SERVES 5

Heat the olive oil in a medium heavy-bottomed saucepan over medium-high heat, add the onion and garlic and cook until soft but not colored. Add the ground beef and cook for 3–4 minutes or until browned. Add the oregano and wine and cook until reduced and almost evaporated. Stir in the tomato paste, ketchup, and chile sauce and cook for a further minute. Add the tomato soup, chicken broth, and a pinch of salt and pepper to taste. Simmer over medium-low heat for 15 minutes (adding more broth if needed, but you don't want it too wet as it's going to be the calzone filling). Stir in the parsley and cooked macaroni and set aside to cool to room temperature.

Place 2 pizza stones in the oven and preheat the oven to 500°F (260°C) or to its highest temperature. Once it has reached the temperature, it will then take about 15 minutes for the pizza stones to heat up.

Lightly dust a clean work surface with semolina or flour, and then roll out each dough into a 6-inch round that is about ⅛ inch thick. Transfer the pizza bases onto squares of parchment paper; this is necessary for transferring the assembled pizzas to the pizza stone. Prick the pizza bases all over with a fork.

Scatter the parmesan evenly over one side of the pizza bases, leaving a ¾-inch border. Add ½ cup of bolognese mixture over the cheese in the calzoni. Fold the other side over the filling and pinch the edges together, pleating to prevent the mixture from escaping. Brush with the beaten egg and sprinkle each with 1 tablespoon of the extra parmesan.

Transfer two calzoni onto the pizza stones. Cook for 8–10 minutes or until golden and crisp. Carefully remove from the oven using a pizza peel or wide spatula and transfer to a cutting board. Repeat for the other calzoni. Serve.

DOWN UNDER OPEN FISH PIE

I know we do some things differently in Australia, and that's why I've developed this open fish pie; to show you that not all things different are bad. This recipe can also be made in a small ovenproof skillet as individual pizzas—roll out dough and use it to line and come just over the side of the pan, top it with the baccala and fish, then mozzarella. Cook until your kitchen has the most enticing aromas through it.

Place two pizza stones in the oven and preheat the oven to 500°F (260°C) or to its highest temperature. Once it has reached the temperature, it will then take about 15 minutes for the pizza stones to heat up.

Combine the snapper with the baccala sauce.

Lightly dust a clean work surface with semolina or flour, then roll out each dough into a 12-inch round, that is about ⅛ inch thick. Transfer the pizza bases onto two squares of parchment paper; this is necessary for transferring the assembled pizzas to the pizza stones. Prick all over with a fork.

Fold in 1 inch of the edge of each pizza round and pleat your way around to form the crust edges (this holds the filling on the pizzas). Each will end up being a 10-inch pizza base.

Sprinkle over the shredded mozzarella, and the torn buffalo mozzarella, then spoon half the fish mixture onto each pizza base.

Transfer the pizzas onto the preheated pizza stones. Cook for 5-10 minutes or until golden and crisp. Carefully remove the pizza from the oven using a pizza peel or wide spatula and transfer to serving plates.

Mix the lemon juice, dijon mustard, and olive oil together in a medium bowl. Add the arugula leaves and gently toss to dress the leaves. Season with salt and pepper. Add to the top of the pizzas and serve.

10½ oz snapper fillet, skinned, boned and cut into sashimi-like slices

1¼ cups baccala sauce (see p 18)

Semolina or all-purpose flour, for rolling

2 × 6-oz pizza doughs (see p 15)

3½ oz shredded mozzarella

2 oz buffalo mozzarella, torn

1 tablespoon lemon juice

1 teaspoon dijon mustard

1 tablespoon olive oil

½ cup wild arugula leaves

Sea salt and freshly ground black pepper

MAKES TWO 10-INCH ROUND PIZZAS

SERVES 2-4

BREAKFAST PIZZA

At my restaurants, we take pizza making very seriously and it shows. We have won best pizza in Australia accolades a number of times, as well as taking out the mantle of Best Pizza in the World at the New York pizza competition. Pizzas are a wonderful meal to serve at home and I believe they can be quite healthy if you don't overload them with poor-quality cheese. It is for this reason that I sometimes make this pizza at home for breakfast. It is fun to make, and eat.

Semolina or all-purpose flour, for rolling

6 oz pizza dough (see p 15)

$\frac{1}{3}$ cup pizza sauce (see p 19)

1 tablespoon chopped fresh flat-leaf (Italian) parsley

$\frac{1}{2}$ cup shredded mozzarella

2 small pork sausages, cooked, sliced diagonally

2 baby roma tomatoes, quartered

Sea salt and freshly ground black pepper

1 free-range egg

Small handful of arugula leaves

$\frac{1}{2}$ teaspoon olive oil

$\frac{1}{4}$ teaspoon lemon juice

3 tablespoons ricotta cheese

MAKES ONE 12-INCH SQUARE PIZZA

SERVES 2

Place a pizza stone in the oven and preheat the oven to 500°F (260°C) or to its highest temperature. Once it has reached the temperature, it will then take about 15 minutes for the pizza stone to heat up.

Lightly dust a clean work surface with semolina or flour, and then roll out the dough into a rough 12-inch square that is $\frac{1}{8}$ inch thick. Transfer the pizza base onto a piece of parchment paper; this is necessary for transferring the assembled pizza to the pizza stone. Prick the pizza base all over with a fork.

Brush the pizza sauce evenly over the pizza base, then scatter over the chopped parsley and shredded mozzarella. Arrange the sliced sausage on the pizza, then the tomato quarters, and season with salt and pepper.

Transfer the pizza onto the preheated pizza stone and cook for 5-10 minutes or until golden and crisp.

Meanwhile, cook the egg in a nonstick skillet with a touch of oil until cooked to your liking. Toss the arugula with the olive oil and lemon juice.

Carefully remove the pizza from the oven using a pizza peel or wide spatula and transfer to a cutting board. Garnish with the fried egg, lightly dressed arugula leaves, dollops of ricotta cheese, and more ground pepper. Serve.

HUEVOS RANCHEROS

I created my version of this wonderful Mexican breakfast dish, huevos rancheros, many years ago for one of my restaurants that serves breakfast. I took the liberty of adding some avocado, sour cream, and lime to freshen it up.

Place two pizza stones in the oven and preheat the oven to 500°F (260°C) or to its highest temperature. Once it has reached the temperature, it will then take about 15 minutes for the pizza stones to heat up.

Lightly dust a clean work surface with semolina or flour, then roll out each dough into a 6-inch round that is 1/8 inch thick. Transfer the pizza bases onto squares of parchment paper; this is necessary for transferring the assembled pizzas to the pizza stones. Prick the pizza bases all over with a fork.

Spread the salsa evenly over the pizza bases, followed by the beans. Sprinkle with the shredded mozzarella. Crack the eggs into separate cups.

Transfer the pizzas onto the preheated pizza stones, then add the eggs to the center of the pizzas. Sprinkle some chopped cilantro and cheddar cheese directly onto the eggs and season the eggs with salt and pepper.

Cook the pizzas for 5–10 minutes or until golden and crisp. Carefully remove the pizza from the oven using a pizza peel or wide spatula and transfer to a serving plate. Top with avocado, sour cream, extra cilantro sprigs, sliced jalapeños, if using, and lime juice. Serve.

NOTE: If using an electric pizza oven, follow the instructions on page 11, adding the cilantro and cheddar with the egg.

Semolina or all-purpose flour, for rolling

2 × 3-oz pizza doughs (see p 15)

4 tablespoons tomato salsa

4 tablespoons canned refried beans

2 oz shredded mozzarella

2 free-range eggs

2 tablespoons chopped fresh cilantro, + extra sprigs, to serve

2/3 cup grated cheddar cheese

Sea salt and freshly ground black pepper

1/2 avocado, sliced

2 tablespoons sour cream or crème fraîche

4 jalapeños, optional

Juice of 1 lime

MAKES TWO 6-INCH ROUND PIZZAS

SERVES 2

APPLE AND RHUBARB PIE WITH MASCARPONE AND ICE CREAM

There is nothing more pleasing than being invited to someone's house for dinner and, at the end of the meal, they offer you a slice of warm homemade apple pie. This recipe cranks it up a notch by adding stewed rhubarb but, more importantly, I have turned it into a pizza, so you can make little individual ones for everyone or make a large one where everyone gets a slice.

1 granny smith apple, peeled, cored, cut into 1 inch dice

1 tablespoon water

1 teaspoon lemon juice

$\frac{1}{4}$ teaspoon ground cinnamon

2 tablespoons superfine sugar

$5\frac{1}{2}$ oz rhubarb, trimmed, washed and cut into 3-inch lengths

1 tablespoon brown sugar

$\frac{1}{8}$ teaspoon baking powder

1 tablespoon rolled oats

2 tablespoons all-purpose flour

$\frac{3}{4}$ oz butter, chilled and diced

$\frac{1}{3}$ cup mascarpone cheese

$\frac{3}{4}$ teaspoon confectioners' sugar, sifted, + extra for dusting

Semolina or all-purpose flour, for rolling

2 × 4-oz pizza doughs (see p 15)

Vanilla ice cream, to serve

MAKES TWO 7-INCH ROUND PIZZAS

SERVES 4–6

Place the apple, water, lemon juice, ground cinnamon, and superfine sugar in a small saucepan. Cover and cook over medium-low heat, stirring occasionally, for about 5 minutes. Add the rhubarb, cover and cook, stirring occasionally, for 8 minutes or until the apple and rhubarb are tender. Set aside to cool to room temperature. Strain to remove any excess liquid.

Place two pizza stones in the oven and preheat the oven to 500°F (260°C) or to its highest temperature. Once it has reached the temperature, it will then take about 15 minutes for the pizza stone to heat up.

Meanwhile, place the brown sugar, baking powder, rolled oats, and flour in a bowl and mix well to combine. Use your fingers to rub the butter into the flour mixture until it resembles coarse breadcrumbs. Set aside. In a small bowl, combine the mascarpone with the confectioners' sugar. Set aside.

Lightly dust a clean work surface with semolina or flour, and then roll out each dough into a 7-inch round that is about $\frac{1}{8}$ inch thick. Transfer the rolled pizza bases onto squares of parchment paper; this is necessary for transferring the assembled pizzas to the pizza stones. Prick the pizza bases all over with a fork.

Spread each pizza base evenly with half the sweetened mascarpone. Top each with half the apple mixture and half the oat crumble mix.

Transfer the pizzas onto the pizza stones and cook for 5–8 minutes or until golden and crisp. Carefully remove the pizza from the oven using a pizza peel or wide spatula and transfer to a cutting board. Dust with the extra confectioners' sugar, and serve with vanilla ice cream.

Chocolate and Hazelnut with Banana and Vanilla Gelato

This is the first dessert pizza I ever toyed around with. I wanted something on the menu that customers couldn't resist. It had to have chocolate, hazelnuts, bananas, honey, ice cream or gelato, and confectioners' sugar. I think this is one of the best pizzas I've ever created, and it's fantastically easy to make yourself. Buy the best quality ice cream or gelato you can to top this special dessert.

Place a pizza stone in the oven and preheat the oven to 500°F (260°C) or to its highest temperature. Once it has reached the temperature, it will then take about 15 minutes for the pizza stone to heat up.

Lightly dust a clean work surface with semolina or flour, and then roll the dough into a 4 × 6-inch oval that is about ⅛ inch thick. Transfer the pizza base onto a piece of parchment paper; this is necessary for transferring the assembled pizza to the pizza stone. Prick the pizza base all over with a fork.

Spread the chocolate-hazelnut paste evenly over the pizza base. Place the sliced banana neatly on top, then the ricotta cheese.

Transfer the pizza onto the preheated pizza stone. Cook the pizza for 5-10 minutes or until golden and crisp. Carefully remove the pizza from the oven using a pizza peel or wide spatula and transfer to a cutting board. Dollop on a scoop of ice cream, and sprinkle over the chocolate shavings and hazelnuts. Drizzle over the honey and dust with confectioners' sugar, if desired, before serving.

Semolina or all-purpose flour, for rolling

4 oz pizza dough (see p 15)

3 tablespoons chocolate-hazelnut paste

1 banana, sliced and coated in lemon juice

1 tablespoon fresh ricotta cheese, broken into pieces

1 scoop vanilla ice cream or gelato, to serve

2 tablespoons chocolate shavings

2 tablespoons toasted, peeled, and chopped hazelnuts

2 teaspoons honey

Confectioners' sugar, for dusting, optional

MAKES ONE 4 X 6-INCH OVAL PIZZA

SERVES 2–4

PECAN PIE PIZZA WITH SALTED CARAMEL SAUCE

Yum, yum, and yum is all that needs to be said about this pizza!

Semolina or all-purpose
flour, for rolling

4 × 4½-oz pizza doughs (see p 15)

⅔ cup pecans

4 tablespoons pure maple syrup

Vanilla ice cream, to serve

Confectioners' sugar, for dusting,
optional

Pinch of sea salt flakes

SALTED CARAMEL SAUCE

⅔ cup superfine sugar

2 tablespoons water

⅔ cup whipping cream

Pinch of sea salt flakes

PECAN BASE

⅔ cup pecans

2 oz unsalted butter, softened

2 oz superfine sugar

1 egg

2 tablespoons all-purpose flour,
sifted

**MAKES FOUR 6-INCH
ROUND PIZZAS**

SERVES 2–4

To make salted caramel sauce, place the sugar and water in a small saucepan over low heat and cook, stirring occasionally, until the sugar has dissolved. Brush the side of the saucepan with a pastry brush dipped in water. Increase the heat to medium and bring to a boil. Simmer for 5-7 minutes or until the sugar starts to turn caramel. Carefully add the cream (it will bubble and spatter violently), stirring constantly until smooth. Stir in the salt. Transfer to a heatproof bowl and allow to cool.

To make the pecan base, grind the pecans in a mortar and pestle until finely ground. Using an electric mixer, cream the butter and sugar in a bowl until pale and fluffy. Add the egg and mix until incorporated in the mixture. Fold in the ground pecans and flour until incorporated. Set aside.

Place two pizza stones in the oven and preheat the oven to 500°F (260°C) or to its highest temperature. Once it has reached the temperature, it will then take about 15 minutes for the pizza stones to heat up.

Lightly dust a work surface with semolina or flour, and roll out each dough into a 4 × 6-inch round that is ⅛ inch thick. Transfer the pizza bases onto squares of parchment paper; this is necessary for transferring the assembled pizzas to the pizza stones. Prick the pizza bases all over with a fork. Spread 3 tablespoons of pecan base evenly over each pizza base, and then lay the whole pecans around the pizza.

Transfer two of the pizzas onto the pizza stones. Cook the pizzas for 5-8 minutes or until golden and crisp. Remove the pizzas from the oven using a pizza peel or wide spatula and transfer to a cutting board. Drizzle with maple syrup, dollop a scoop of ice cream in the center, drizzle with salted caramel sauce, dust with confectioners' sugar (if using), and sprinkle a little salt over the caramel sauce. Repeat with the remaining pizzas and serve.

NOTE: If using an electric pizza oven, follow the instructions on page 11, and cook for 10 minutes.

BERRIES WITH VANILLA CHANTILLY CREAM AND RICOTTA CHEESE

Recent research has named blueberries a superfood due to their nutrient-dense makeup. This is great news as berries are delicious. This pizza could also be made in a pie shape by folding up the edges, or made into a great calzone.

To make the berry compote, place the blueberries, sugar, and lemon zest in a saucepan over medium-high heat. Bring to a boil. Take off the heat and add the remaining berries. Gently stir through. Set aside to cool.

Place two pizza stones in the oven and preheat the oven to 500°F (260°C) or to its highest temperature. Once it has reached the temperature, it will then take about 15 minutes for the pizza stones to heat up.

To make the flapjack mix, sift the flour and baking powder into a bowl, then add the sugar. In a separate bowl, mix the egg yolks and milk together, then slowly whisk into the dry ingredients. Break up the ricotta cheese and add to the mix. Whisk the egg whites in a separate bowl until stiff peaks form, then fold them into the ricotta mixture. Set aside.

Lightly dust a work surface with semolina or flour, then roll out each dough into a 6-inch round that is $1/8$ inch thick. Transfer the pizza bases onto squares of parchment paper; this is necessary for transferring the assembled pizzas to the pizza stones. Prick the pizza bases all over with a fork. Evenly spread $1/3$ cup of flapjack mix onto the pizza bases, leaving a $1/2$-inch border. Transfer two pizza bases onto the pizza stones. Cook the pizzas for 5-10 minutes or until golden and crisp.

Meanwhile, whisk the cream, sugar, and vanilla to soft peaks. Set aside.

Carefully remove the pizzas from the oven using a pizza peel or wide spatula and transfer to a cutting board. Drizzle each pizza with 1 tablespoon maple syrup, add a dollop of the cream mixture, then spoon on $1/6$ of the berry compote. Serve with a sprig of mint. Repeat for the other pizzas.

NOTE: If using an electric pizza oven, follow the instructions on page 11, flipping the pizza after 8 minutes and cooking for a further minute.

Semolina or all-purpose flour, for rolling

6 × 3-oz pizza doughs (see p 15)

$1^{1}/_{4}$ cups whipping cream

1 tablespoon confectioners' sugar, sifted

$1/2$ vanilla bean, seeds scraped

$1/2$ cup pure maple syrup

Mint sprigs, to serve

BERRY COMPOTE

$5^{1}/_{2}$ oz blueberries

$3/4$ cup + 1 teaspoon superfine sugar

Finely grated zest of 2 lemons

4 oz raspberries

4 oz strawberries, hulled, quartered

FLAPJACK MIX

2 tablespoons all-purpose flour

$1/2$ teaspoon baking powder

1 teaspoon superfine sugar

2 egg yolks

$1/4$ cup milk

$2^{1}/_{2}$ oz fresh ricotta cheese

2 egg whites

MAKES SIX 6-INCH ROUND PIZZAS

SERVES 3-6

INDEX

weldon**owen**

415 Jackson Street, Suite 200, San Francisco, CA 94111
Telephone: 415 291 0100 Fax: 415 291 8841
www.wopublishing.com

Weldon Owen is a division of

BONNIER

First published in the United States in 2012

Concept designer: Alexandra Zeigler
Layout designer: Emma Gough
Photographer: Brett Stevens
Stylist: Reuben Crossman
Assistant Stylist: Miriam Steenhauer
Food editor: Sonia Greig
Editor: Daniela Bertollo
Production: Alexandra Gonzalez
Project Editors: Livia Caiazzo and Claire Grady

Color separations by Splitting Image Colour Studio, Melbourne, Australia.

10 9 8 7 6 5 4 3 2 1

Library of Congress Control Number: 2011941261

ISBN: 978-1-61628-168-7